RAISING MENTALLY STRONG AND SECURELY ATTACHED KIDS

THE 5-PART PARENTING BLUEPRINT TO RAISE RESILIENT, SOCIALLY SUCCESSFUL, AND EMOTIONALLY INTELLIGENT CHILDREN

VIVIAN WHITMORE

© Copyright 2025. Vivian Whitmore - All rights reserved.
The content contained within this book may not be reproduced, duplicated or transmitted without direct written permission from the author or the publisher.

Under no circumstances will any blame or legal responsibility be held against the publisher, or author, for any damages, reparation, or monetary loss due to the information contained within this book, either directly or indirectly.

Legal Notice:
This book is copyright protected. It is only for personal use. You cannot amend, distribute, sell, use, quote or paraphrase any part, or the content within this book, without the consent of the author or publisher.

Disclaimer Notice:
Please note the information contained within this document is for educational and entertainment purposes only. All effort has been executed to present accurate, up to date, reliable, complete information. No warranties of any kind are declared or implied. Readers acknowledge that the author is not engaged in the rendering of legal, financial, medical or professional advice. The content within this book has been derived from various sources. Please consult a licensed professional before attempting any techniques outlined in this book.

By reading this document, the reader agrees that under no circumstances is the author responsible for any losses, direct or indirect, that are incurred as a result of the use of the information contained within this document, including, but not limited to, errors, omissions, or inaccuracies.

Contents

BOOK ONE

Introduction	7
Chapter 1: Understanding Attachment	10
Chapter 2: Building Emotional Connections	18
Chapter 3: Navigating the Digital Landscape	26
Chapter 4: Enhancing Daily Practices	33
Chapter 5: Avoiding Common Pitfalls	42
Conclusion	51

BOOK TWO

Introduction	55
Chapter 1: Foundations of Secure Attachment	57
Chapter 2: Teaching Resilience as a Skill	64
Chapter 3: Emotional Intelligence for Improved Connections	64
Chapter 4: Mindful Parenting and Breaking Generational Patterns	71
Chapter 5: The Complete Parent's Toolkit for Raising Socially Thriving Kids	82
Conclusion	88

BOOK THREE

Introduction	93
Chapter 1: What Is Emotional Intelligence?	95
Chapter 2: Building Emotional Awareness	104
Chapter 3: Teaching Emotional Regulation	112
Chapter 4: Developing Empathy and Compassion	122
Chapter 5: Social Skills for Emotional Intelligence	133
Conclusion	139

BOOK FOUR

Introduction	143
Chapter 1: Recognizing Generational Patterns	146
Chapter 2: Healing Your Inner Child	153
Chapter 3: Mindful Parenting in Action	163
Chapter 4: Transforming Discipline Into Teaching	173
Chapter 5: Building a New Family Legacy	185
Conclusion	197

BOOK FIVE

Introduction	203
Chapter 1: The Foundations of Social Success	206
Chapter 2: Strategies to Help Children Overcome Social Challenges	217
Chapter 3: Teaching Empathy and Gratitude	231
Chapter 4: Mastering Communication Skills	236
Chapter 5: Preparing for Real-World Social Success	246
Conclusion	261
References	265

Book One

Introduction

What does it mean to truly connect with a child? In a world filled with digital distractions and mounting pressures, the most profound gift we can offer isn't found in toy stores or wrapped in colorful paper—it's about being present every day, in the gentle constancy of our presence and the warmth of our unconditional love. These seemingly ordinary interactions—a reassuring smile during that first wobbly step, a comforting embrace after a playground tumble, or simply being there to witness a proud achievement—form the foundation of what psychologists call attachment, a powerful force that shapes how children view themselves and navigate their world.

In this exploration of attachment theory, we'll discover how these early bonds create blueprints for emotional resilience, healthy relationships, and lifelong well-being. Whether you're a parent juggling the countless demands of raising a child, an educator fostering connection in your classroom, or a mental health professional guiding families toward stronger relationships, understanding the science of attachment will transform how you approach these crucial early years.

Think of attachment as an invisible safety net that gives children the courage to explore, learn, and grow. Every time a baby reaches for their caregiver's familiar face, every instance a toddler checks back while venturing toward a new playground friend, and each moment a child seeks comfort after a disappointment—these are not just fleeting interactions but vital building blocks of emotional security.

For parents, this understanding offers a refreshing perspective amid the often overwhelming landscape of child-rearing advice. You don't need elaborate activities or picture-perfect moments; your consistent, attuned presence will support your child throughout their life. It's about finding the extraordinary in ordinary moments—transforming routine tasks like grocery shopping into adventures of discovery, or turning bedtime routines into precious opportunities for connection.

Educators and childcare professionals will discover how attachment theory illuminates the complex dynamics they observe daily in their classrooms. That child who seems perpetually glued to your side? That student who rarely participates in group activities?

Through the lens of attachment theory, these behaviors take on new meaning, allowing you to create environments that nurture both security and learning. You become more than a teacher—you're an emotional architect, designing spaces where children feel safe risks, make mistakes, and flourish.

For mental health professionals, attachment theory provides a framework for understanding family relationships. Like a map of the emotional landscape your clients navigate, this understanding enhances your therapeutic approach, enabling more effective support for families working to strengthen their bonds. Whether you're helping parents connect with their teenagers or guiding families through trauma healing, attachment theory offers invaluable insights for fostering healing and growth.

The impact of early attachment extends far beyond childhood, influencing how individuals approach relationships and handle life's challenges throughout their years. Think of it as tending a garden—the care and attention you invest today determines how your children will bloom tomorrow. While this might sound daunting, our approach focuses on practical, achievable strategies that naturally integrate into daily life. Perfect parenting isn't the goal; rather, it's the small, consistent actions that create lasting change.

In the chapters that follow, we'll explore research-backed insights and practical techniques for fostering secure attachments. Through real-world examples and hands-on exercises, you'll develop skills to

- create meaningful connections in everyday moments, from morning rushes to bedtime snuggles, understanding how these small interactions build lasting security.
- recognize and respond to attachment-related behaviors, learning to read the subtle language of emotional needs.
- design environments that promote emotional security across different settings—homes, classrooms, and therapeutic spaces.
- support healthy relationship development through various developmental stages, adapting your approach as children grow.

You'll hear inspiring stories from parents who've discovered how understanding attachment transformed their relationships with their children. Teachers will share how this knowledge revolutionized their classrooms, and therapists will describe how attachment-based approaches helped families rebuild stronger connections.

These aren't just success stories—they're roadmaps for your own journey in nurturing secure, confident children.

Each chapter builds upon the last, offering practical tools you can implement immediately. We'll address common challenges like separation anxiety, behavioral issues, and relationship repairs with compassion and clarity, showing how daily interactions can become opportunities for deepening connection.

Welcome to this journey of understanding attachment—your guide to strengthening the bonds that shape future generations. Think of this book as your companion in the adventure of nurturing secure, confident children. Together, we'll explore how understanding and nurturing these crucial early connections can transform lives, one relationship at a time. Let's begin this exploration of building stronger, more resilient relationships with the children in your life.

Chapter One

UNDERSTANDING ATTACHMENT

It's 8:45 p.m., and I'm sitting cross-legged on my son's bedroom floor, reading Where the Wild Things Are for what feels like the millionth time. In this simple moment, I witnessed the practical application of attachment theory, namely the profound impact of being a consistent, loving presence in a child's life. These everyday interactions, from bedtime stories to morning hugs, form the bedrock of emotional security that shapes a lifetime of relationships. While the concept might sound academic, its reality plays out in living rooms, playgrounds, and kitchen tables across the world every day.

Attachment Theory

Attachment theory, pioneered by John Bowlby and Mary Ainsworth, reveals how early caregiver relationships shape our emotional development. When caregivers consistently respond to a child's needs with warmth and understanding, they activate biological systems—including the release of oxytocin—that build trust and emotional resilience.

This isn't just about creating happy moments; it's about laying the groundwork for a lifetime of healthy relationships and emotional well-being.

The brain science behind attachment reveals how early relationships shape neural development in profound ways. When children experience consistent, nurturing care, it affects multiple brain systems simultaneously. The stress response system, controlled by the hypothalamic-pituitary-adrenal (HPA) axis, develops more effectively, leading to better cortisol regulation and enhanced ability to handle stress. This results in more balanced emotional responses throughout life. Additionally, the social areas of the brain strengthen, particularly the neural pathways responsible for empathy and emotional understanding. The mirror neuron system, amygdala, and orbitofrontal cortex all develop more robustly, enhancing a child's ability to form and maintain relationships.

Now that we understand the scientific foundation of attachment, let's explore how these patterns manifest in everyday interactions.

Secure vs. Insecure Attachment in Action

Understanding what secure attachment looks like in daily life can transform how we interpret children's behaviors and needs. A securely attached child might confidently explore a playground, looking for reassurance from their parents from time to time. They recover relatively easily from upset with caregiver support, and they're comfortable seeking help when needed. This balance of independence and connection creates a dance of exploration and safety that characterizes healthy development.

Insecure attachment often manifests in ways that are difficult to deal with for both children and their caregivers. Some children can be excessively clingy, while others appear surprisingly indifferent to their caregivers. These children often struggle with emotional regulation and peer relationships, and they find it difficult to trust others and find support when they need it. Understanding these patterns helps us respond more effectively to children's needs, rather than just reacting to their behavior.

As we consider these different attachment styles, take a moment to reflect on the patterns you observe in your own relationships with children. What behaviors do you notice that might indicate secure or insecure attachment?

The Long-Term Impact

Securely attached children typically develop stronger emotional regulation skills and better social relationships. They tend to perform better academically and are more resilient when dealing with challenges. These children often grow into adults who maintain healthy relationships, manage stress effectively, and approach life with confidence and optimism.

Understanding these long-term effects helps us appreciate why investing in secure attachment today creates ripples that extend far into the future. Let's explore how different caregivers can nurture these vital connections.

For Parents, Educators, and Mental Health Professionals

Parents

To foster secure attachment, you need to be consistently present in your child's life. This means responding reliably to your child's emotional needs, creating predictable routines that provide a sense of safety, and offering comfort during times of distress. It's about staying present during daily interactions, even when they feel mundane or repetitive. Each response to a cry, each moment of eye contact during feeding, each patient listening to a long-winded story about recess contribute to building secure attachment.

Educators

Creating a classroom environment that feels safe and predictable helps students develop trust in their learning environment. Teachers who recognize attachment-related behaviors can respond more effectively to students' needs, maintaining consistent, warm responses that support healthy development. When educators understand attachment theory, they're better equipped to support both struggling students and those who are thriving.

Mental Health Professionals

Understanding attachment patterns helps therapists support parents in developing more secure relationships with their children. This might involve helping parents explore their own attachment histories, identifying patterns that influence their parenting, and developing strategies for building stronger family bonds.

As we consider these different roles, reflect on your own position in children's lives. How can you adapt these principles to better support the children in your care?

Cultural Considerations

Attachment patterns vary significantly across cultures, challenging the idea of a universal standard. In Japan, co-sleeping into early school years nurtures valued interdependent bonds, while West African communities often foster multiple strong attachments within extended family networks. The Gusii people of Kenya maintain minimal eye contact with their babies—a practice that might seem distant by Western standards but creates healthy attachment within their cultural context. Meanwhile, many Asian cultures prioritize physical dependence longer while expecting earlier emotional self-regulation.

Take a moment to consider your own cultural heritage: What attachment practices were passed down through your family? How do these align with or differ from what you've learned about attachment theory? Which cultural traditions would you like to preserve or adapt in your approach to building secure attachments?

Case Studies

Consider three-year-old Tommy, who demonstrates secure attachment in his relationship with his mother, Sarah. He confidently explores the playground while checking back with her periodically, showing the perfect balance of independence and connection. When he falls and gets hurt, he seeks comfort from his mother but can quickly return to play once soothed. His behavior shows how secure attachment creates a stable foundation for exploring the world.

In contrast, four-year-old Lisa displays anxious attachment patterns with her father, Mark. She clings to him and resists exploring, even in familiar settings. Her extreme distress during separations and difficulty engaging with peers reflect how insecure attachment can limit a child's social and emotional development. Similarly, three-year-old Devon shows avoidant attachment behaviors, appearing indifferent when his parent leaves or returns and rarely seeking comfort when upset. His tendency to play alone and resist physical affection demonstrates how early attachment patterns can influence social interaction styles.

Following these children over time reveals the lasting impact of these early attachment patterns. By age seven, Tommy makes friends easily and shows confidence in new situations, demonstrating how secure attachment supports healthy social development.

Lisa, at age eight, continues to struggle with separation anxiety and peer relationships, while Devon, at age six, maintains emotional distance and has difficulty expressing feelings. However, it's important to note that with consistent, nurturing care and appropriate support, insecure attachment patterns can be modified over time, showing the remarkable plasticity of the developing brain and the ongoing opportunity for positive change.

Now that we've explored these real-world examples, let's examine your own experiences with attachment. In the following exercise, we'll reflect on patterns you've observed and consider how you might apply these insights to strengthen your relationships with children.

REFLECTION EXERCISE: UNDERSTANDING YOUR ATTACHMENT STYLE

Part 1: Personal Attachment Patterns

Think about your own attachment patterns by answering these questions. Here's an example response to help guide your reflection:

Example response: When my daughter is upset about not being invited to a birthday party, my first reaction is to jump into problem-solving mode ("We can plan something fun instead!"). I notice I feel anxious and want to fix the situation quickly. Reflecting back, this mirrors how my own mother responded to my childhood disappointments—always trying to find immediate solutions rather than sitting with the emotions. Now I'm learning to first validate my daughter's feelings ("It hurts to feel left out") before moving to solutions.

Your Reflection Questions

1. How do you typically respond when your child is upset?
    - What's your first reaction?
    _____
    - What emotions come up for you?
    _____
    - How does this compare to how you were comforted as a child?
    _____

Part 2: Weekly Connection Tracker

Week of: _____

Connection Level Guide

1 = Minimal interaction
- Example: Quick goodbye during morning rush
- Example: Brief check-in about homework completion

2 = Brief but pleasant exchange
- Example: Shared laugh over breakfast
- Example: Quick cuddle before bedtime
- Example: Short conversation about school day

3 = Good conversation/moment
- Example: Extended discussion about friend conflict at school
- Example: Working together to make dinner
- Example: Playing a board game together

4 = Deep connection
- Example: Heart-to-heart about fears or worries
- Example: Collaborative problem-solving session
- Example: Meaningful shared experience like teaching a new skill

5 = Exceptional bonding moment
- Example: Breaking through a communication barrier
- Example: Supporting through a significant challenge
- Example: Sharing a profound moment of understanding or joy

DAILY MOMENTS & REFLECTIONS

Monday Sample Entry: What happened? We had an impromptu dance party while cleaning up dinner dishes.

How did it make you feel? Joyful and connected—loved seeing my son laugh so freely.

Type of interaction: Activity connection level: 4. Location: Kitchen. Time of day: 6:30 PM.

Your entry: What happened?

_____

_____

How did it make you feel?

_____
_____
_____

Type of interaction (circle): Conversation / Activity / Support / Shared Experience connection level (1-5): __ Location: _____ Time of day: _____

[Continue format for Tuesday-Sunday]

SAMPLE WEEK ENTRIES TO GUIDE YOUR REFLECTION

Tuesday example: What happened? Sat together during thunderstorm, talked about weather fears. How did it make you feel? Trusted, protective, touched by their vulnerability. Type: Support connection level: 4, Location: Living room couch, Time: 9:00 p.m.

Wednesday example: What happened? Morning meltdown over wrong socks, stayed calm and validated feelings. How did it make you feel? Initially frustrated, then proud of maintaining patience. Type: Support connection level: 3. Location: Bedroom. Time: 7:15 a.m.

Thursday example: What happened? Shared stories about our days during walk home from school. How did it make you feel? Engaged and curious about their world. Type: Conversation connection level: 3. Location: Neighborhood sidewalk. Time: 3:30 p.m.

REFLECTION PROMPTS FOR WEEKLY REVIEW

1. What patterns do you notice in your most meaningful connections?
    - Time of day: Are there particular times when deeper connections occur?
    - Location: Which spaces foster better connections?
    - Type: What kinds of interactions lead to stronger feelings of connection?
2. Looking at your connection levels:
    - What made the higher-rated moments special?

- What circumstances contributed to lower-rated interactions?
- How might you create more opportunities for deeper connection?

3. Sample Insights from Weekly Tracking: "I noticed our best connections happen during unplanned moments when I'm fully present rather than trying to force interaction." "Bedtime consistently offers opportunities for meaningful conversation when we're both relaxed and unhurried."

4. "Car rides provide unexpected chances for deep discussions—something about the side-by-side positioning seems to help."

Monthly Review Questions:

1. What themes emerged in your most meaningful moments?
2. How have your responses to your child's emotions evolved?
3. What new strategies have you discovered for fostering connection?
4. Which times/places/activities consistently nurture stronger bonds?

Remember: There's no "perfect" pattern of connection. The goal is to understand your unique relationship dynamics and build awareness of opportunities for meaningful interaction within your daily routine.

Key Takeaways

- ❏ Attachment theory explains how consistent, warm responses from caregivers build trust and emotional resilience in children, physically shaping brain development and stress regulation systems.
- ❏ Secure attachment creates a healthy balance of independence and connection, while insecure attachment manifests as either excessive clinginess or apparent indifference with emotional regulation difficulties.
- ❏ The benefits of secure attachment extend throughout life, including stronger emotional regulation, better social relationships, higher academic performance, and greater resilience to challenges.
- ❏ Cultural variations exist in healthy attachment practices, and while early patterns influence development, insecure attachment can be modified through consistent, nurturing care and self-reflection.

Chapter Two

BUILDING EMOTIONAL CONNECTIONS

Maya couldn't help but smile as she watched three-month-old Sophia's face light up during their daily "good morning" routine. What had started as a simple peek-a-boo game had evolved into an elaborate ritual of gentle touches, silly faces, and a made-up song that Maya had unconsciously created one sleepless night. Every morning, without fail, Sophia would greet her mother's familiar face with increasingly energetic kicks and a gummy grin that seemed to grow wider each day.

Today was no different, except that Maya noticed something new. As she reached the final verse of their special song, a part where she always touched Sophia's nose with a gentle "boop", her daughter's tiny hands reached up in anticipation, already prepared for their shared moment.

This simple morning ritual illustrates the power of consistent, loving interactions in building strong emotional bonds. Let's explore how we can intentionally create these meaningful connections from the very beginning.

Prenatal and Early Bonding Strategies

Building emotional bonds with your baby can begin even before birth through prenatal bonding. Parents can practice mindfulness during pregnancy by taking quiet time each day to focus on their baby, using gentle breathing exercises and visualization to create early connections.

After birth, skin-to-skin contact becomes a crucial bonding tool. When you hold your newborn against your bare chest, it does more than create a cozy moment. It helps stabilize their heart rate, breathing, and temperature. This close contact triggers the release of oxytocin, often called the "love hormone," which strengthens the bond between parent and child and helps develop secure attachments.

Establishing consistent routines provides babies with a sense of security and predictability in their world. Regular schedules for activities like bathing, napping, and playing help babies understand what to expect throughout their day. These patterns aren't just about keeping time they help babies develop emotional regulation skills and create a stronger parent-child bond through reliable, repeated interactions.

Responsive caregiving ties everything together. When parents promptly and consistently address their baby's needs, whether it's hunger, discomfort, or the desire for attention, they're teaching their child that their feelings matter. This attentive approach helps babies develop trust and emotional intelligence.

As we consider these early bonding strategies, take a moment to reflect on your own experiences. What routines have you naturally developed with your baby? How do they respond to different types of interaction?

Cultural Considerations for Trust and Connection

Cultural practices play a vital role in shaping how parents and children form emotional bonds. Different cultures around the world offer unique approaches to building these connections, from Asian traditions that emphasize family interdependence to Indigenous practices that embrace community-based child-rearing.

Traditional activities like storytelling serve as powerful tools for building trust and passing down cultural wisdom. When families gather to share stories, they create opportunities for meaningful connection while teaching values and life lessons across generations. Similarly, both celebratory rituals (like naming ceremonies) and daily routines (such as shared meals and bedtime stories) help create stable, predictable moments that strengthen family bonds.

Take a moment to consider your own cultural heritage: What bonding practices were passed down through your family? Which traditions would you like to preserve or adapt for your own children? How might you incorporate practices from other cultures that resonate with your parenting values?

Implementing Emotional Bonding Techniques

Consider Sarah's morning routine with her baby Thomas. She begins each day with a warm "Good morning, sunshine!" in a gentle, sing-song voice. Thomas responds with bright eyes and a smile, already anticipating their special time together. Sarah continues by saying, "Let's wake up our body!" while giving Thomas a gentle massage on his hands and feet. His excited kicks tell her he's fully engaged in their morning ritual. They finish with a playful game of peek-a-boo, Thomas giggling and reaching out as Sarah playfully asks, "Where's my baby? There you are!"

Physical affection plays a crucial role in emotional bonding. Regular hugs, kisses, and gentle touches reassure children of their parents' love and support their emotional well-being. Even as children grow older and seem to resist affection, these gestures remain important for maintaining connection.

Now that we understand the theory behind emotional bonding, let's put these ideas into practice with some concrete exercises.

BUILDING EMOTIONAL CONNECTIONS: PRACTICE EXERCISES

Exercise 1: Creating Your Morning Ritual

Consider how Lisa developed her morning routine with six-month-old Emma. She started by observing Emma's natural rhythms, noticing how her daughter was most responsive right after her first feeding, especially to high-pitched, playful voices. She then created a sequence combining Emma's favorite elements: a special good morning song, gentle butterfly kisses, and a game where Lisa pretends Emma's toes are little piggies going to market. The consistency of this routine has helped Emma start each day feeling secure and loved.

Exercise 2: Empathetic Response Training

Picture a common bedtime scenario: Four-year-old Marcus is fighting sleep, tears streaming down his face as he insists, "I don't want to go to bed!" His father Michael demonstrates effective empathetic response by kneeling to Marcus's level and speaking softly: "I hear that you're feeling frustrated about bedtime." When Marcus protests that he's not tired, Michael acknowledges his feelings: "It can be hard to stop playing and go to sleep. Would you like to choose which story we read together?" This simple offer of choice helps Marcus feel heard and gives him some control over the situation. As Marcus calms slightly and asks for the dinosaur book, Michael reinforces their connection: "The dinosaur book is a great choice. Let's get cozy and read it together."

Exercise 3: Daily Connection Moments

Think about the natural opportunities for connection throughout your day. After school pickup, for instance, can become a special moment of reconnection. When eight-year-old Olivia runs to her mother Claire's open arms, Claire often says, "I missed you today!" They share their special handshake, a ritual they created together that makes Olivia feel special and seen. These small moments of physical connection—morning cuddles, impromptu dance breaks while making dinner, or gentle back rubs during bedtime stories—make us feel loved and secure throughout the day.

Remember that building emotional connections is a journey, not a destination. Each small moment of connection adds up to create a strong, lasting bond with your child. As you practice these exercises, notice what feels natural and authentic for your relationship, and adapt them to fit your family's unique style.

BUILDING EMOTIONAL BONDS: YOUR PERSONAL CONNECTION PLAN

This worksheet is designed to help you create meaningful rituals and moments of connection with your child. Just like Maya and baby Sophia's morning routine or Lisa and Emma's special wake-up ritual, you can develop your own unique bonding experiences.

Part 1: Observe & Notice

Take a few days to simply notice when your child seems most responsive and engaged with you. What brings the biggest smiles or most focused attention?

Time of day:

_____

What we were doing:

_____
_____

My child's response:

_____
_____

Time of day:

_____

What we were doing:

_____
_____

My child's response:

_____
_____

Time of day:

_____

What we were doing:

_____
_____

My child's response:

_____
_____

When does your child seem most connected to you?

_____

_____

Part 2: Create Your Special Ritual

Based on what you observed, design a simple two to three-minute ritual to do regularly with your child.

Best time for our ritual: _____

Elements to include: (check all that will work for you)

☐ a special greeting or phrase

☐ gentle touch (like "butterfly kisses" or a special handshake)

☐ a simple song or rhyme

☐ a game (like peek-a-boo or "this little piggy")

☐ a moment of eye contact and smiling

☐ Other: _____

Our ritual sequence:

_____

_____

Part 3: Connection Throughout the Day

Identify three everyday moments you can transform into brief connection points:

Morning moment:

_____

_____

Daytime moment:

_____
_____

Evening moment:

_____
_____

Part 4: Weekly Reflection

After trying your ritual for one week:

What worked well?

_____
_____

What would I like to adjust?

_____
_____

How did my child respond?

_____
_____

How did these moments of connection make me feel?

_____
_____

Remember

❏ Keep it simple. Even 30 seconds of focused connection matters.
❏ Be consistent but flexible. You should adapt as your child grows.
❏ Notice what brings you both joy. The best rituals feel good for everyone.

Each small moment of connection adds up to create a strong, lasting bond with your child.

Key Takeaways

❑ Building emotional bonds with children starts early through consistent, loving interactions like skin-to-skin contact, responsive caregiving, and establishing predictable routines that provide security.

❑ Creating personalized rituals, strengthens parent-child connections and helps children develop trust and emotional intelligence.

❑ Cultural practices and traditions play a significant role in bonding, from storytelling to daily routines, and parents can adapt these to fit their unique family values.

❑ Small, intentional moments of connection throughout the day, morning greetings, physical affection, empathetic responses to emotions, accumulate to create lasting emotional bonds that support a child's development.

Chapter Three

NAVIGATING THE DIGITAL LANDSCAPE

Sarah watched her six-year-old Emma staring longingly at the tablet on the bookshelf, its screen time already used up for the day. "But Mom, just five more minutes? Lily gets to watch videos all afternoon!" Emma pleaded with her best puppy-dog eyes.

Instead of an immediate "no," Sarah sat beside her daughter on the floor. "You know what? I sometimes feel the same way about my phone. It's like it has magical powers that make us want to keep watching, isn't it?"

Emma's surprise turned to interest as Sarah pulled out some building blocks. "Want to build something amazing together instead? I bet we can make a castle that even YouTube princesses would be jealous of."

As Emma began stacking blocks, her tablet cravings momentarily forgotten, Sarah smiled. These transitions weren't always smooth, but each small win felt like progress in balancing their digital and real worlds.

Sarah's approach demonstrates how empathy and creativity can transform challenging technology moments into opportunities for connection. Let's explore how we can develop similar strategies for our own families.

Screen Time Boundaries and Healthy Habit Modeling

Think of screen time limits like a daily schedule; they work best when everyone knows what to expect. For young kids, start with simple rules like "tablets only after homework" or "no screens an hour before bedtime." The key is consistency: When your seven-year-old knows they get 30 minutes of game time after finishing their reading, there's less room for negotiation and drama.

Consider how the Martinez family handles their technology boundaries: Eight-year-old Miguel knows that after completing his math practice, he can spend 20 minutes playing his favorite educational game. His sister Carmen, age six, looks forward to their "Saturday Morning Cartoon Time" a special hour when the whole family watches and discusses shows together.

As we think about setting boundaries, consider your own family's relationship with technology: What digital habits from your childhood influence your current approach to parenting? How do your cultural background and family values shape your views on screen time?

Making Rules Together

Turn rule-making into a family project. Sit down with your kids and ask: "When do you think would be the best time for watching videos?" or "How can we make sure we still have time for playing outside?" When kids help create the rules, they're more likely to follow them.

The Thompson family found success with their "tech token" system. Ten-year-old Jamie earns tokens through activities like reading chapters in his book or helping fold laundry. Each token equals 15 minutes of game time, making screen time feel like a reward rather than a restriction. His younger sister Mia loves the colorful chart where they track their tokens, turning it into a game itself.

Walking the Talk

Kids notice everything, especially when we're not practicing what we preach. If you want your children to develop healthy tech habits, show them what that looks like. The Chen family demonstrates this beautifully: During dinner time, parents Alice and David place their phones in a special "phone home" basket. Their children, seeing this consistent example, naturally follow suit without complaint.

Now that we've explored different approaches to managing technology, let's consider how we can use it positively to strengthen family bonds.

Using Technology Positively to Enhance Parental Bonds

Digital technology, when used thoughtfully, can strengthen parent-child relationships in meaningful ways. Take the Wilson family's "Digital Discovery Sundays" each week, twelve-year-old Sophia and her dad spend an hour learning coding together through an interactive program, sharing victories and working through challenges as a team.

As we consider these positive uses of technology, reflect on your own family's digital interactions: What technology-based activities bring you closer together? How might you transform passive screen time into active family engagement?

FAMILY TECHNOLOGY BALANCE WORKBOOK

Now that we've explored various approaches to family technology use, let's create a personalized plan for your family.

Exercise 1: Family Tech Agreement

Here's how the Baker family completed their agreement:

Device-free times: "Meals, homework hours (3-5 p.m.), and after 8 p.m." Device-free zones: "Bedrooms and dining room". Approved apps/games: "Educational games list posted on fridge, parent-approved YouTube channels". Daily screen time limits: "60 minutes on school days, 90 minutes on weekends". Consequences: "Reduced next day's time by amount of overage".

Exercise 2: Technology Impact Log

Sample entry from the Patel family:

Monday:

- mood after device use: 3/5 (Ryan was frustrated when game time ended)
- quality of sleep: 4/5 (no devices an hour before bed helped)
- family interactions: More (played board game instead of videos)
- physical activity: 45 minutes (evening walk while phones stayed home)

Exercise 3: Alternative Activities Bank

The Rodriguez family's favorite alternatives:

Indoor activities:

- family board game championships
- living room fort building
- indoor scavenger hunts
- cooking challenges

Outdoor activities:

- nature photography walks
- backyard obstacle courses
- family soccer matches
- garden tending time

Creative activities:

- family band practice
- art gallery creation
- story writing workshops
- DIY craft projects

Exercise 4: Weekly Tech Check-In

Example from the Johnson family's check-in:

❑ **What worked well:** "Morning routine without phones helped everyone get ready faster".

❑ **What needs adjustment:** "Weekend screen time needs clearer boundaries".

❑ **Next week's goals:** "Try device-free Sunday afternoons"

Remember that finding the right technology balance is an ongoing journey unique to each family. Use these exercises as starting points, adapting them to fit your family's needs, values, and cultural context. The goal isn't perfection but progress in creating meaningful connections in our digital age.

Navigating Digital Challenges: Real-World Solutions

Every family's journey toward healthy technology use comes with unique challenges. Let's explore some common scenarios and practical solutions that have worked for real families.

Managing Tech-Related Tantrums

The Garcia family struggled with nine-year-old Lucas's meltdowns whenever screen time ended. After several difficult weeks, they discovered a simple but effective technique: the five-minute warning. "Lucas, you have five minutes left before we turn off the tablet," became their standard practice, giving him time to reach a natural stopping point in his game. They also created a special "transition box" filled with non-screen activities he enjoyed—drawing supplies, LEGO sets, and puzzle books—that were only available immediately after screen time ended.

"The transition box completely changed our evenings," explains Lucas's mother, Elena. "Instead of dreading the end of screen time, he now looks forward to what activity he'll choose next."

Handling Peer Pressure Around Technology

Eleven-year-old Zoe came home from school upset because "everyone else" had the latest social media app that her parents didn't allow. The Wright family addressed this challenge by scheduling a special "tech talk" dinner where Zoe could share her feelings. They listened empathetically before explaining their concerns about the app's age-appropriateness.

"Instead of just saying no, we found alternatives," explains Zoe's father. "We helped her set up video calls with friends and even created a private photo-sharing group with family members where she could practice digital communication skills in a safer environment."

Dealing With Technology During Family Gatherings

The O'Neill family noticed that holiday gatherings had become silent affairs with everyone glued to separate screens. They created a "tech holiday tradition" where all devices go into a decorated basket during family events. To ease the transition, they introduced engaging group activities like a family trivia game with questions about their shared history and traditions.

"The first fifteen minutes are always a bit uncomfortable," admits grandmother Patricia. "But soon everyone remembers how to talk to each other, and the laughter returns."

Tech-Positive Parenting: Finding the Balance

It's easy to view technology as the enemy, but balanced tech-positive parenting recognizes both its benefits and limitations. Consider these principles as you develop your family's approach:

Digital Literacy as a Family Value

The Kim family sees technology education as essential to their children's future. Rather than simply restricting access, they focus on teaching critical skills. Weekly "fact-check challenges" have become a favorite activity, where family members present information found online and others research to verify its accuracy.

"We're not just teaching them how to use technology safely," says father Min-jun. "We're teaching them how to think critically about the information they consume."

Embracing the Learning Potential

Preschool teacher and mother of three, Aisha Williams, suggests looking for the educational value in children's technology interests. When her son became obsessed with a particular video game, she helped him create a physical map of the game world, incorporating math skills and spatial reasoning into his passion.

"The key is connection, not restriction," Aisha explains. "When I showed interest in his game world instead of just limiting it, it became something we could share and learn from together."

The Power of "Tech Sabbaticals"

The Goldstein family instituted a monthly "tech sabbatical" weekend where all screens stay off from Friday evening through Sunday morning. Initial resistance gave way to anticipation as these weekends became filled with family hikes, elaborate cooking projects, and rediscovered board games.

"Our kids now look forward to these weekends," shares mother Rachel. "They've realized how much more we laugh and connect when screens aren't competing for our attention."

Remember that technology balance isn't about eliminating screens but about creating intentional spaces—both with and without technology—where your family can thrive together. The most successful approaches combine clear boundaries with genuine curiosity about the digital world your children inhabit, creating a family culture where meaningful connection remains the priority in both digital and physical spaces.

Key Takeaways

- ❑ Establishing consistent, clear screen time boundaries works best when children participate in creating the rules, making them more likely to follow limits they helped design.
- ❑ Parents must model healthy technology habits themselves, as children notice when adults don't practice what they preach about digital boundaries.
- ❑ Technology can positively enhance family bonds when used intentionally for shared activities like coding projects, digital discovery sessions, or creative collaborations.
- ❑ Successful strategies for managing technology challenges include transition techniques (five-minute warnings, alternative activity boxes), addressing peer pressure with empathy, and creating tech-free family traditions while still embracing digital literacy as a valuable skill.

Chapter Four

ENHANCING DAILY PRACTICES

The familiar sound of tiny feet brought Alex's morning smile as four-year-old Jamie appeared, clutching his elephant. It was time for their 7:15 "special time."

As the toaster dinged, Alex began their daily ritual. "What shape should we make your toast into today, Chef Jamie?"

"Star!" Jamie exclaimed from his kitchen helper stool. "And can Ellie watch?" he added, setting his elephant on the counter.

While they turned ordinary toast into a stellar creation, Alex reflected on how this simple routine had grown from a solution for a picky eater into precious moments of connection that brightened their whole day.

"Remember when you used to hide under the table at breakfast time?" Alex asked.

Jamie giggled, sprinkling raisins on his masterpiece. "That was when I was little. Now I'm the breakfast helper!"

Alex and Jamie's morning ritual shows how simple routines can transform challenging moments into opportunities for connection. Let's explore how we can create similar meaningful rituals in our own families.

Creating Rituals for Safety and Emotional Stability

Establishing consistent rituals is like wearing your favorite cozy sweater—it just feels right and comfortable. When it comes to children, these rituals can be key in creating a sense of safety and emotional security. Kids without a predictable routine might feel like they're living in a house of bouncy castle chaos, not knowing what's coming next.

Take a moment to reflect on the rituals from your own childhood: What practices from your cultural background made you feel safe and connected? How might you adapt these traditions for your family today?

Morning and Bedtime Routines

Consider how the Kim family transformed their hectic mornings into peaceful connections. Seven-year-old Min-ji and her mother share a special wake-up song, followed by getting dressed "like dancing butterflies." This routine, inspired by Korean lullabies from Min-ji's grandmother, has eliminated morning battles while preserving cultural connections.

Family Meals

Think of these as the ultimate Wi-Fi for human connection. The Garcia family turns dinner prep into a cultural celebration, with nine-year-old Steven learning his grandmother's empanada recipe while sharing stories about his day. These moments become more than meal preparation, they're bridges between generations and cultures.

Now that we've explored different types of rituals, let's consider how mindfulness can deepen these connections.,

Mindful Moments

Think of teaching kids about emotions like teaching them any other skill. The Smith family demonstrates this beautifully in their evening "feeling circle," where six-year-old Priya leads the family in taking three deep breaths before each person shares their day's emotions using their native language and English, creating a rich bilingual emotional vocabulary.

PRACTICE EXAMPLES

The feeling break

Parent: I noticed you seem quiet today. Would you like to share what you're feeling?

Child: I'm worried about my presentation tomorrow.

Parent: That sounds hard. When I had to present at work last week, I felt nervous too. What would help you feel more prepared?

The notice game

Parent: I spy something that makes me feel peaceful...

Child: The wind in the trees!

Parent: Yes! How does it make you feel when you watch the leaves dance?

These mindful practices create space for emotional awareness. Let's build on this foundation with active listening and gratitude.

Practices For Active Listening And Gratitude

The Thompson family demonstrates active listening during their "cozy corner chats." When eight-year-old Sarah shares about a playground conflict, her father sits at her level, maintaining eye contact, and reflects back what he hears: "It sounds like you felt left out when your friends played without you. That must have been really hard."

GRATITUDE PRACTICE EXAMPLES

Morning gratitude

Parent: I'm grateful for your morning hugs. They make my heart smile.

Child: I'm thankful for pancake Saturdays and when you make funny shapes!

Evening reflection

Parent: What made your heart happy today?

Child: Playing soccer with Lisa! She taught me a special trick her mom showed her.

FAMILY GRATITUDE JOURNAL EXAMPLES

The Johnson family keeps a shared journal where each member writes or draws

- something that made them laugh.
- someone who helped them.
- a challenge they overcame.
- a tradition they love.

As we implement these practices, remember that each family's journey is unique. The goal isn't perfection but connection.

Reflection Exercise: Creating Your Family's Ritual Map

Take a moment to consider:

- What daily moments could become special rituals?
- How can you incorporate elements of your cultural heritage?
- What practices align with your family's natural rhythm?

The Power of Family Rituals

Family rituals serve as anchors in our busy lives, creating moments of connection that children remember long into adulthood. These aren't necessarily elaborate traditions but often the simplest, most consistent practices become the most meaningful.

Think about Maya and Sophia's morning "boop" ritual from our earlier example. What began as a spontaneous interaction evolved into a cherished daily connection that both mother and daughter anticipate. Your family can create similar touch points throughout your day.

Identifying Ritual Opportunities

Consider these potential ritual moments in your family's schedule:

Transition times

- morning wake-ups (How could the first moments of the day set a positive tone?)
- after-school reunions (What would make your child feel truly welcomed home?)
- bedtime wind-downs (What calming elements help your family transition to rest?)

Shared spaces

- meal preparations (Could cooking together become a time for stories or songs?)

- car rides (What simple games or conversations could transform travel time?)
- outdoor moments (How might regular nature connections become meaningful rituals?)

Cultural connections

- family heritage practices (What traditions did you experience as a child?)
- holiday celebrations (How can these honor your roots while creating new meaning?)
- language rituals (Could bilingual families incorporate special phrases or sayings?)

Sample Family Ritual Plan

Morning

- special wake-up song from parent's childhood
- morning greeting in family's heritage language
- brief mindful moment with a shared stretch or deep breath

Meals

- sharing of one "rose" (good thing) and one "thorn" (challenge)
- table setting ritual where each family member has a special responsibility
- cultural grace or gratitude practice before eating

Evening

- cultural stories or lullabies before bed
- "worry basket" where children can symbolically place their concerns
- gentle touch ritual like a special handshake or forehead kiss

Weekly

- Sunday family game night featuring games from different cultures
- Friday "family choice" dinner where a different member selects the meal each week
- Saturday morning pancake breakfast with special family recipes

Adapting to Different Ages and Stages

Remember that rituals should evolve as your family grows:

For babies and toddlers: Focus on sensory-rich, simple interactions like special songs, gentle touch games, and consistent language cues.

For school-age children: Incorporate more active participation and choice—let them suggest variations or take leadership roles in family rituals.

For adolescents: Create space for independence while maintaining connection. Perhaps a weekly one-on-one ritual with each parent or a special way to acknowledge growing maturity.

Getting Started: Your Three-Step Approach

1. **Observe:** For one week, notice when your family seems most naturally connected. When do conversations flow? When does everyone seem relaxed and engaged?

2. **Experiment:** Choose just one or two potential ritual moments to focus on first. Keep them simple and sustainable.

3. **Evolve:** After a month, discuss what's working. What do family members look forward to? What feels forced? Adjust accordingly.

Remember that building meaningful family rituals is a journey of discovery. Start small, stay consistent, and let your family's unique personality shine through each tradition you create. The most powerful rituals often emerge organically from what already brings your family joy.

What matters most isn't perfection but presence—being fully engaged in these special moments of connection that, over time, become part of your family's shared story.

The Ripple Effect of Family Rituals

When we create meaningful rituals with our children, the benefits extend far beyond the moment itself. Like ripples in a pond, these consistent practices create waves of positive impact that touch every aspect of family life.

Building Resilience Through Connection

The Velasquez family discovered this power during a particularly challenging year. When eight-year-old Luis's father was deployed overseas, their nightly video call ritual became an emotional anchor. Even with a twelve-hour time difference, Luis and his mother maintained their "Three Good Things" practice, each sharing three positive moments from their day before his father shared his own.

"Some nights I could barely think of anything good," Luis's mother shared. "But knowing we had this tradition pushed me to notice small blessings the neighbor who shoveled our walkway, Luis's laughter during dinner, the cardinal that visited our bird feeder. These tiny moments of gratitude carried us through."

Families who maintain consistent rituals during times of stress demonstrate greater resilience and emotional well-being.

Honoring Your "Good Enough" Rituals

Perhaps you're reading this and thinking about all the picture-perfect family traditions you haven't established. Take a deep breath. Remember that the most meaningful rituals aren't Instagram-worthy productions but consistent moments of genuine connection.

The Walsh family learned this lesson during a hectic season of life with three children under five. Their "family dinner" often looked like organized chaos. "Some nights dinner was cereal or sandwiches eaten in shifts between activities," explains Michelle Walsh. "But we never skipped our 'squeeze hands' tradition where we all link hands in a circle before eating and give three squeezes to symbolize 'I-love-you.' That simple five-second ritual kept us connected even when everything else felt rushed."

Your family's rituals don't need to be elaborate or perfect. The "good enough" ritual done consistently creates more connection than the elaborate tradition that happens only when conditions are ideal.

When Rituals Need Reimagining

As families evolve, so too must their rituals. When the Chen family welcomed their second child, their leisurely Sunday morning pancake tradition suddenly felt impossible with a newborn's unpredictable schedule. Rather than abandoning the tradition entirely, they reimagined it.

"We switched to 'Pancake Day' which could happen any day of the week when energy and timing aligned," explains Wei Chen. "We kept the essential elements—our special family recipe, everyone helping according to ability, and eating together—but released the expectation about when it had to happen."

This flexibility allowed their meaningful tradition to adapt rather than disappear during a new family stage. Consider which elements of your rituals are essential and which can evolve as your family changes.

The Unexpected Joy of Emergent Rituals

Some of the most meaningful family rituals are never planned but emerge organically from life's unexpected moments. The Abrams family discovered this when a power outage led to an impromptu living room campout. Flashlight shadow puppets and storytelling by candlelight were such a hit that "Blackout Night" became a monthly tradition with the lights intentionally turned off, devices put away, and imagination taking center stage.

Pay attention to those magical, unplanned moments of connection in your family. Sometimes the rituals that most perfectly fit your family's personality are the ones you never could have designed.

Your Invitation: One Small Step

As we conclude our exploration of family rituals, consider this your invitation to take one small step. You don't need to revolutionize your family schedule overnight. Instead:

1. **Notice** one moment this week where connection happens naturally.

2. **Name** it as special: "I love our Saturday morning snuggles" or "Our walk home from school is my favorite part of the day".

3. **Nurture** it with your attention and presence, allowing it to develop its own rhythm and meaning.

Remember that in twenty years, your children won't recall if the house was perfectly clean or if dinner was homemade every night. What they'll treasure are the consistent threads of connection that made them feel seen, known, and deeply loved—the simple, repeated rituals that told them, day after day: "You belong here. You matter to us. This family is your forever home.

Key Takeaways

- ❑ Consistent family rituals create emotional safety and stability for children, serving as anchors that transform ordinary moments into meaningful connections.
- ❑ The most powerful rituals aren't elaborate traditions but often simple, consistent practices that occur during natural transition points like mornings, mealtimes, and bedtimes, incorporating elements of cultural heritage and mindfulness.
- ❑ Family rituals build resilience, especially during challenging times, by providing predictable moments of connection that help family members notice positive experiences even amidst difficulties.
- ❑ Successful rituals should evolve with your family's changing needs and can emerge organically from unexpected moments; the goal isn't perfection but presence—creating consistent touch points of connection that children will remember into adulthood.

Chapter Five

AVOIDING COMMON PITFALLS

Three-year-old Lily stood at the bottom of the playground slide, her small hands gripping the metal rails as she contemplated her ascent. Her mother, Rachel, hovered nearby, every muscle tensed and ready to act. This was their daily dance at the park. Lily testing her boundaries, Rachel fighting the urge to lift her daughter up the ladder.

Today was different, though. As Lily placed one foot on the first rung, Rachel took a deep breath and stepped back, just half a step. She watched as her daughter carefully climbed, pausing briefly at each level. When Lily reached the top, she didn't immediately slide down as usual. Instead, she sat there for a moment, surveying her kingdom from this new height. Her face broke into a smile that illuminated the entire playground.

"Look, Mommy! I'm tall like a giraffe!" Lily called out, pride radiating from every word. In that moment, Rachel realized her daughter's greatest triumph wasn't just reaching the top of the slide it was discovering she could do it on her own. The real challenge hadn't been Lily's climb, but Rachel's own journey in learning to step back, finding that delicate balance between protecting her child and fostering independence.

Rachel and Lily's story illustrates the delicate balance many parents face between protection and independence. Let's explore how we can navigate this journey while honoring our cultural values and family traditions.

Balancing Supportive Parenting With Fostering Independence

Consider how the Lee family approaches independence: six-year-old Ming learns to use chopsticks at his own pace, his mother resisting the urge to switch him to a fork when he struggles. This patience honors their cultural traditions while building Ming's confidence and motor skills.

Take a moment to reflect: What independence-building practices from your cultural background have influenced your parenting? How might these traditions guide your approach to fostering independence?

Practical Approaches

EXAMPLE SCENARIO

Making breakfast

Parent: Would you like to help make your oatmeal this morning?

Child: Can I do it myself?

Parent: Let's do it together first. You can measure the oats while I handle the hot water.

Next time

Child: I remember! First oats, then water.

Parent: That's right! I'll watch while you measure.

Building Problem-Solving Skills

The Smith family uses "pause and plan" moments:

Sofia (age 7): I can't reach my jacket!

Parent: What could you use to help you reach it?

Sofia: Maybe... the stepstool?

Parent: That's great thinking! Would you like me to spot you while you try?

Now that we understand the foundation of supportive independence, let's explore how our own upbringing influences our parenting style.

Breaking Cycles of Emotional Neglect

Consider the Singh family's transformation of traditional practices. While Priya grew up hearing "don't cry" when upset, she now validates her son Arjun's emotions while maintaining their cultural values.

Traditional vs. Responsive Approach

Scenario: Child is upset about losing a game

Traditional response: Stop crying, it's just a game.

Transformed response: In our family, we feel our feelings AND show strength. It's okay to be disappointed. Would you like to take some deep breaths together?

Scenario: Child is upset about losing a game

Traditional response: Stop crying, it's just a game.

Transformed response: In our family, we feel our feelings and show strength. It's okay to be disappointed. Would you like to take some deep breaths together?

Let's practice transforming common responses into emotionally supportive moments while respecting cultural values.

Encouraging Gradual Independence

The Taylor family's "Step-by-Step" approach combines traditional values with modern independence:

Morning routine example

Age 4-5

- Choose between pre-selected outfits.
- Help make bed with parent.
- Put away pajamas.

Age 6-7

- Select weather-appropriate clothes.
- Make bed independently.
- Pack school snack with guidance.

Age 8-9

- Plan outfit the night before.
- Complete morning hygiene routine.
- Pack full lunch with supervision.

Cultural Independence Activities

The Wong family incorporates traditional responsibilities in their daily routine such as

- learning to serve tea to elders
- helping prepare festival foods
- participating in family ceremonies

Let's create your family's independence-building plan, combining cultural traditions with age-appropriate responsibilities.

Practical Independence Exercises

Now that we've explored various approaches, let's develop concrete strategies for your family.

Daily Skills Builder

Kitchen Independence Example

Step 1: Observation (Day 1-2)

- Child watches parent make simple sandwich.
- Parent narrates each step.
- Discuss safety rules.

Step 2: Assisted practice (Day 3-5)

- Child spreads butter with parent guiding hand.
- Child chooses fillings from safe options.
- Parent handles any cutting needed.

Step 3: Supervised independence (Week 2)

- Child makes sandwich while parent watches.
- Parent stays nearby for safety.
- Celebrate effort and problem-solving.

Step 4: Modified independence (Week 3+)

- Child makes own lunch snacks.
- Parent checks in periodically.
- Discuss any challenges or proud moments.

Weekly Independence Challenge

Choose one new skill to develop each week:

1. Personal care: brushing teeth thoroughly
2. Home responsibility: setting the table
3. Social skills: ordering own food at restaurants
4. Academic: packing school bag

Remember that fostering independence is a gradual process unique to each family and culture. The goal isn't to push children into independence but to support their natural journey toward self-reliance while maintaining strong family bonds.

Celebrating the Journey: Small Steps Toward Confident Independence

As we reflect on Rachel and Lily's playground moment and the various approaches families take toward fostering independence, it's worth remembering that this journey isn't a straight line. Some days, your child will surprise you with their capability; other days, they may seek more support. Both experiences are valuable parts of growing up.

Finding Your Family's Rhythm

The Jackson family discovered this when eight-year-old Marcus suddenly refused to order his own food at restaurants after doing so confidently for months. Instead of pushing or expressing disappointment, his father simply said, "I'm happy to help today. Sometimes we all need a break from being brave."

Two weeks later, Marcus volunteered to order again. When his father later asked what changed, Marcus explained, "I just needed to know it was okay if I wasn't ready sometimes."

This flexibility—allowing children to move between independence and dependence without judgment—creates the emotional safety needed for genuine confidence to develop.

Cultural Wisdom in Modern Parenting

Many traditional cultures have understood the importance of gradual independence for centuries. The Navajo concept of "walking in beauty" emphasizes harmony between protection and growth. Elders historically involved children in community work according to their developmental readiness, not arbitrary age milestones.

Yara, a mother of Lebanese heritage, incorporates this wisdom by teaching her daughters to make traditional tabbouleh. "At five, my younger daughter just helps wash the parsley. My eight-year-old chops vegetables with a small knife while I supervise. My mother taught me the same way, increasing responsibility gradually while we worked together. These aren't just cooking lessons—they're lessons in becoming."

Technology and Independence: Finding Balance

Today's parents face challenges previous generations didn't—particularly regarding technology. The Estevez family established a technology independence ladder for their children:

"We started with closely supervised tablet time when they were younger," explains Carlos. "As they demonstrated responsibility, we gradually extended their digital independence. Now our teenagers manage their own screen time within agreed boundaries. The conversations about digital citizenship actually strengthened our cultural values about respect and responsibility." The key was making technology part of their independence journey rather than treating it as separate from other developmental skills.

When Children Need Extra Support

Some children naturally seek independence, while others need more encouragement. When six-year-old Zoe showed extreme reluctance to try anything new, her mothers worried. "We realized Zoe needed smaller steps than the parenting books suggested," says Leila. "We broke down each new skill into tiny pieces, celebrating each micro-achievement."

They created the "Brave Board" where Zoe placed stickers for each small step toward independence—wearing a new hair clip, asking a question at the library, or trying a food with an unfamiliar texture. "The progress seemed invisible day-to-day, but looking back over months, the transformation was remarkable. She needed her own timeline, not ours."

Building a Village of Support

Supporting independence doesn't mean parents must do everything alone. The Thomas family taps into their community network, with eleven-year-old Jordan learning different skills from various trusted adults.

"Jordan's uncle teaches him woodworking, our neighbor shows him gardening, and his afterschool program covers cooking basics," explains his mother. "This 'village approach' connects him to our community while building diverse skills. It resembles how children traditionally learned in our culture—from many adults, not just parents."

This approach reduces pressure on any single parent to teach everything while exposing children to various teaching styles and expertise.

Celebrating Interdependence

Perhaps most importantly, fostering independence isn't about raising children who don't need others. Rather, it's about raising children who understand when and how to seek connection, support, and collaboration.

The Kim family emphasizes this distinction in their evening conversations. "We don't just ask how our children showed independence today," says Jun-ho. "We also ask how they helped someone else or accepted help themselves. We want them to value interdependence—knowing when to stand alone and when to reach for support."

This balanced perspective honors many cultural traditions that value community connections alongside personal capability.

Your Family's Unique Path

As you continue supporting your child's growing independence, remember that comparison is rarely helpful. Your family's journey will reflect your unique values, your child's temperament, and the specific challenges and opportunities in your lives.

The Wu family discovered this when their daughter struggled with separation anxiety at preschool drop-off, long after other children entered happily. "We worried we'd done something wrong," remembers Lin. "Then her teacher helped us see that each child has their own timetable for emotional independence. We needed patience, not pressure."

By adjusting their expectations and creating a special goodbye ritual, they eventually celebrated their daughter's confident entry into the classroom—on her timeline, not anyone else's.

The Unexpected Gift

Perhaps the most beautiful aspect of supporting our children's independence is how it transforms us as parents. When four-year-old Elijah finally mastered pouring his own milk after weeks of practice (and many spills), his father Devon found himself unexpectedly emotional.

"Watching him concentrate so hard on that simple task made me realize my role was shifting," Devon shares. "Each small independence he gains changes our relationship—not diminishing it, but evolving it. We're both growing through this process."

In those quiet moments of stepping back—whether it's watching your child climb a playground ladder, make their first sandwich, or walk into school without looking back—we're not just witnessing their independence. We're discovering a new dimension of parenthood: the profound joy of seeing our children become themselves, one small brave step at a time.

Key Takeaways

- ❑ Finding the balance between protection and independence creates opportunities for children to develop confidence through their own achievements.
- ❑ Independence should be fostered gradually with age-appropriate responsibilities, breaking skills into manageable steps while honoring cultural values and family traditions.
- ❑ Emotionally supportive parenting transforms traditional approaches by validating children's feelings while teaching resilience, allowing them the flexibility to move between independence and dependence without judgment.
- ❑ True independence isn't about raising children who don't need others but developing their ability to recognize when to stand alone and when to seek connection, celebrating interdependence within family and community.

Conclusion

In the grand adventure of parenting, education, and therapy, understanding secure attachment is like discovering the ultimate life hack. It's the foundation that helps children grow into resilient adults who can navigate life's challenges with confidence and emotional intelligence.

For parents, educators, and mental health professionals, implementing secure attachment principles comes down to three key actionable steps:

Create Consistent Safe Spaces

Whether you're a parent managing morning routines or a teacher handling classroom conflicts, consistency will help you get ahead. Set up predictable environments where children know they can express their feelings without judgment. This means responding to emotional outbursts with calm understanding rather than frustration, and establishing reliable routines that children can count on. When a child knows their emotional world is valid and supported, they develop the confidence to explore, fail, and try again.

Build Emotional Intelligence Through Modeling

The magic happens when we demonstrate healthy emotional responses ourselves. Instead of hiding our challenges, we can narrate our problem-solving process: "I'm feeling frustrated right now, so I'm going to take three deep breaths and think about this differently." This shows children that emotions aren't scary—they're valuable signals that help us understand ourselves and others. Practice naming emotions together, explore coping strategies, and celebrate small victories in emotional regulation.

Foster Resilience Through Guided Independence

Break the cycle of overprotection by creating opportunities for supported risk-taking. Let children attempt challenging tasks while staying nearby as their safety net. Whether it's a toddler learning to climb stairs or a teenager navigating social conflicts, your role is to offer guidance while allowing them to develop their own problem-skills.

Remember, you're not aiming for perfection—you're building a foundation of security one interaction at a time. Every time you respond with patience instead of frustration, every moment you spend actively listening to a child's concerns, you're strengthening the bonds that will support them throughout their lives.

Let's turn these insights into action. Choose one strategy to implement today, and watch as small, consistent efforts bloom into lasting, secure attachments. Your journey toward creating stronger connections starts with this moment—and you've got everything you need to succeed.

The beauty of secure attachment work lies in its cumulative effect. Like drops of water filling a bucket, each positive interaction adds to a child's sense of security. Even on difficult days when patience runs thin or schedules fall apart, remember that repair is just as important as prevention. Showing a child how to mend a relationship after a miscommunication teaches them that connections can weather storms and emerge stronger. Document your progress by noting moments when you see a child's confidence growing or when they navigate a difficult emotion with new skills. Share these observations with other caregivers to create a consistent support network. By committing to this attachment-focused approach, you're not just solving today's behavioral challenges but you're investing in a lifetime of healthy relationships and emotional wellbeing for the children in your care.

Book Two

Introduction

Every parent has experienced that moment at the playground watching their child climb higher than ever before, hearts caught between pride and concern. These seemingly simple moments of childhood are powerful windows into how our children approach challenges, building the emotional muscles they'll use throughout their lives.

Parenting today feels more complex than ever. Between managing packed schedules, navigating school demands, and trying to raise well-adjusted kids in an increasingly complicated world, many of us find ourselves lying awake at night, questioning our choices. Yet even these moments of doubt reflect our deep commitment to getting it right.

This guide offers a practical approach to one of parenting's most important tasks: raising children who are both emotionally intelligent and mentally strong. Rather than adding to your already full plate, we'll explore how to transform everyday moments into opportunities for emotional growth. Those bedtime battles? They're chances to teach patience and self-regulation. That playground conflict? It's an opportunity to develop problem-solving skills and empathy.

At the heart of this approach is understanding how secure emotional bonds shape a child's development. When children feel safely connected to their caregivers, they develop the confidence to explore, take risks, and bounce back from setbacks. Think of it like a safety net—knowing it's there allows a trapeze artist to attempt increasingly challenging moves. Similarly, children who feel securely attached are more likely to embrace challenges rather than shy away from them.

The practical strategies we'll explore work within your existing routine. You don't need to schedule extra activities or buy special equipment. Instead, we'll look at how to make the most of daily interactions—from morning rushes to evening wind-downs. Each chapter builds on the last, offering clear, implementable steps that fit real family life.

Consider how children learn to handle frustration. Instead of immediately stepping in when your child struggles with a puzzle or homework assignment, you'll learn how to offer just enough support to keep them engaged while allowing them to develop their own problem-solving skills. This balance, namely knowing when to help and when to step back is crucial for building resilience.

Creating an environment where emotional intelligence flourishes doesn't require perfect parenting. Our occasional missteps can become powerful teaching moments when handled with honesty and grace. When we acknowledge our own mistakes and show how to make amends, we teach our children that challenges are growth opportunities rather than signs of failure.

Throughout this book, you'll find real-life examples from families facing the same challenges you do. Their stories illustrate how small changes in approach can lead to significant improvements in children's emotional resilience. You'll see how other parents have transformed power struggles into cooperation, anxiety into confidence, and resistance into engagement.

The skills your children develop through this approach extend far beyond childhood. They're building the emotional foundation they'll need for future relationships, career challenges, and perhaps their own parenting journeys. When children learn to understand and manage their emotions early in life, they're better equipped to handle whatever challenges life presents.

Remember, this journey isn't about achieving perfection—it's about progress. Each small step you take toward more emotionally aware parenting builds upon the last. Whether you're just starting to explore these concepts or looking to refine your approach, you'll find practical, actionable strategies to support your child's emotional development.

Are you ready to transform your parenting journey? Let's explore how to create an environment where your child can develop the emotional tools they need to face life's challenges with confidence and resilience. Together, we'll turn those playground moments from nerve-wracking experiences into celebrations of growth and capability.

Chapter One

FOUNDATIONS OF SECURE ATTACHMENT

Kelley watched from the kitchen window as her four-year-old daughter Emma tentatively approached the towering jungle gym at the park. Just yesterday, Emma had refused to climb higher than the first rung, clinging to Kelley's leg like a koala. Today was different, though. After a reassuring glance back at her mother, who offered an encouraging smile and a thumbs-up, Emma began to climb.

Halfway up, she froze, her small fingers gripping the metal bars tightly. Kelley resisted the urge to rush over, instead calling out softly, "You've got this, sweetie! I'm right here if you need me."

That was all Emma needed; to know that her safety net was nearby. With renewed determination, she scrambled to the top, her face breaking into a triumphant grin. As Emma celebrated her victory with a princess wave from her new perch, Kelley thought about how far they'd come. The countless bedtime stories, the patient responses to midnight fears, the consistent "welcome home" hugs after preschool—all these small moments had woven together to create something powerful. Emma wasn't just climbing a jungle gym; she was testing her wings, secure in the knowledge that her mother's love was as reliable as gravity.

Attachment Theory Essentials and Application in Parenting

This everyday scene illustrates the heart of attachment theory—how children develop emotional strength through consistent, supportive relationships with their caregivers. Just as Emma needed her mother's presence to attempt that climb, all children need a secure base from which to explore their world. Research pioneers Bowlby and Ainsworth discovered that this security manifests in different attachment styles, each shaping how children approach life's challenges.

Secure attachment looks like this in everyday life:

- The child confidently tries new activities at the playground, knowing mom or dad is nearby.
- A kindergartener comfortably says goodbye at school drop-off, trusting their parent will return.
- A teenager shares both successes and failures, knowing they'll receive support either way.

The impact of secure attachment shows up in real situations:

- When faced with a difficult math problem, securely attached kids are more likely to ask for help instead of giving up.
- During conflicts with friends, they're better at expressing feelings and finding solutions.
- When trying new activities, they show resilience by bouncing back from initial failures.

Creating secure attachment is about consistent, responsive parenting:

- You respond when your toddler falls down, but letting them get back up on their own.
- You listen to your child's school day stories without immediately trying to fix every problem.
- You set reliable routines while being flexible when needed (like adjusting bedtime for special occasions).

Building Trust and Avoiding Generational Trauma

Building secure attachment becomes more complex when parents carry their own emotional burdens, particularly generational trauma. Like an unwelcome family heirloom, patterns of anxiety, depression, or attachment issues can be passed down through generations, affecting how we respond to our children's needs. Understanding these patterns is crucial for breaking the cycle.

Think of healing generational trauma as cleaning out an old suitcase filled with inherited emotional patterns. It requires honest self-reflection and often professional support. Through therapy, journaling, or other healing practices, parents can develop healthier emotional responses, creating a more secure environment for their children. This work isn't just personal growth—it's an investment in your child's emotional future.

Building trust involves more than just promising ice cream on the weekends (though that certainly doesn't hurt). Consistent routines create a predictable environment where children feel safe. When your child shares their experiences, practice active listening—making eye contact, nodding, and responding in ways that show genuine interest, even in playground drama.

Breaking generational trauma requires patience and dedication, much like assembling IKEA furniture without instructions. It involves:

- being honest about family history and accepting that relatives may have been sources of trauma
- seeking professional support to create safe spaces for exploring and addressing trauma roots
- developing awareness of trauma signs and symptoms
- implementing positive parenting techniques
- fostering healthy communication
- prioritizing self-care practices

Impact on Child Development

The effects of secure attachment extend far beyond childhood. Studies show that securely attached children develop stronger stress management skills and healthier relationships throughout life (Groh et al., 2014). When faced with challenges, they're more likely to seek help appropriately, express emotions effectively, and bounce back from setbacks—it's like giving your child an emotional compass that will guide them through life's journey.

Children with secure attachments become more confident to explore their world, knowing they have a cozy emotional safety net back home. They're the adventurers of the playground—fearlessly swinging from monkey bars and bravely diving into friendships! Their ability to regulate emotions develops naturally, like having an internal emotional thermostat that helps them move from upset to calm with growing ease.

fearlessly swinging from monkey bars and bravely diving into friendships! Their ability to regulate emotions develops naturally, like having an internal emotional thermostat that helps them move from upset to calm with growing ease.

For parents, educators, and caregivers, encouraging secure attachment means creating consistent, responsive environments where children feel safe to explore and express themselves. This doesn't require perfection—in fact, showing how to handle mistakes gracefully is itself a valuable lesson. Instead, aim for reliability in your responses and routines, while remaining flexible enough to adapt to your child's changing needs.

Remember Emma on the jungle gym? That moment exemplifies the power of secure attachment in action. Through daily acts of emotional support—bedtime stories, active listening, consistent presence—you build the foundation your child needs to face their own challenges with confidence. Whether it's climbing higher, trying new experiences, or navigating relationships, they'll know they have a secure base to return to, just like Emma knew her mother was there, watching and supporting, ready to celebrate each new achievement.

MY TRUST AND COURAGE JOURNAL

Part 1: My Support Team

Just like Emma had her mom cheering her on, you have special people in your life who support you. Let's make a list of your cheerleaders!

Draw or write about three people you trust to support you when you try new things:

1. _____ helps me by _____

2. _____ helps me by _____

3. _____ helps me by _____

Part 2: My Brave Moments

Think about a time when you did something that felt scary at first (like Emma climbing the jungle gym).

What did you want to try?

What made it feel scary?

_____
_____

Who helped you feel brave?

_____
_____

How did you feel after you did it?

_____
_____

Draw a picture of yourself being brave in this moment!

Part 3: My Confidence Building Blocks

Color in a block each time you do one of these brave things:

- ☐ asked for help when I needed it
- ☐ tried something new
- ☐ shared my feelings with someone I trust
- ☐ got back up after making a mistake
- ☐ helped someone else feel brave

Part 4: My Safety Net Messages

Write down encouraging words that help you feel brave (like Emma's mom saying, "You've got this!"):

When I'm nervous, I can tell myself:

_____
_____

When I need help, I can say:

_____
_____

When I make a mistake, I remember:

_____
_____

Part 5: My Next Adventure

What's something new you'd like to try?

I want to try:

_____

Small steps I can take:

Who can help me?

_____
_____

How will I celebrate when I do it?

_____
_____

Being brave doesn't mean you're not scared. It means trying even when you feel scared! Just like Emma climbing the jungle gym, you can do amazing things with a little courage and support from people who care about you.

Weekly Check-In

At the end of each week, write or draw

- ❑ one thing I did that made me proud.
- ❑ one person who helped me.
- ❑ one way I helped someone else feel brave.

Key Takeaways

❏ Secure attachment, illustrated by Kelley providing encouragement without intervening as Emma climbed the jungle gym, creates a foundation for children to explore confidently while knowing their caregiver remains a reliable safety net.

❏ The effects of secure attachment extend beyond childhood, developing stronger stress management skills, healthier relationships, and the ability to regulate emotions—essentially giving children an "emotional compass" for life.

❏ Breaking cycles of generational trauma requires honest self-reflection, professional support when needed, and consistent parenting practices that build trust through reliable routines and responsive interactions.

❏ Building courage in children involves celebrating brave moments, creating a support network, developing positive self-talk, and breaking challenges into manageable steps—recognizing that bravery isn't the absence of fear but taking action despite it.

Chapter Two

TEACHING RESILIENCE AS A SKILL

Eight-year-old Marcus stared at his half-finished science project, tears welling up. The paper mache volcano he'd spent hours crafting had collapsed on one side, creating what looked more like a lopsided mountain than the majestic volcano he'd imagined. His first instinct was to crumple the whole thing and give up.

Then he remembered the "Pause and Plan" technique Ms. Silverman had taught their class. Taking a deep breath, he closed his eyes and counted to five just like they practiced during morning circle time. When he opened them again, his shoulders relaxed slightly, and the catastrophic feeling began to ebb. "What would a scientist do?" he whispered, echoing his teacher's favorite question. Scientists make mistakes all the time, he remembered. That's how they learn. With renewed determination, Marcus grabbed his supplies and began examining the collapse, not as a failure, but as a puzzle to solve.

As his mom watched from the doorway, she smiled, remembering how differently this scene would have played out just a few months ago. The meltdowns and giving up had transformed into something else—not an absence of frustration, but a growing ability to navigate through it. Marcus was developing his resilience, one challenge at a time.

Incorporating Neuroplasticity Concepts and Emotional Regulation

Marcus's story illustrates a fundamental principle of brain development: Every challenge is an opportunity for growth. Think of a child's brain as a busy city under constant construction, where each new experience builds neural pathways. This concept of neuroplasticity or "brain flexibility" explains why practices like the "Pause and Plan" technique become more effective with repetition.

Just as Marcus learned to pause before reacting to his volcano's collapse, children can develop emotional regulation skills through consistent practice. Here's how this brain science translates into practical strategies:

The "Weather Report Method" helps children understand the temporary nature of emotions:

- Ask them to describe their emotional weather: "Is it stormy? Cloudy? Sunny?"
- Help them recognize that like weather, feelings change and move through.
- Create a daily check-in routine to track their emotional climate.

Building on this foundation, we can introduce the "Superhero Strategy" for overwhelming moments:

- Stand in a power pose like their favorite superhero.
- Take three deep "superhero breaths".
- Ask themselves: "What would [favorite superhero] do right now?"

These aren't just coping techniques, they're building blocks for resilience, strengthening neural pathways with each use.

Fostering a Growth Mindset and Self-Efficacy

The transformation in Marcus's approach to his volcano challenge demonstrates the power of a growth mindset. Instead of seeing the collapse as a failure, he reframed it as a puzzle to solve, a crucial shift in perspective that builds both resilience and problem-solving skills.

To nurture this mindset in daily life

- ❏ Replace "I can't" with "I can't yet".
- ❏ Celebrate effort over outcome: "You tried three different ways to solve that!"
- ❏ Model resilience by handling your own setbacks with grace.

This approach creates an "Explorer's Mindset" where mistakes become discoveries and challenges become opportunities. When children see their parents and teachers embrace this perspective, they're more likely to adopt it themselves.

REFLECTION ACTIVITY: LOOKING BACK TO GUIDE FORWARD

Just as Marcus's mom reflected on his progress, understanding our own journey with setbacks can help us better support our children. This structured reflection exercise builds on the principles we've discussed and helps connect theory to personal experience.

Step 1: Remember a Setback

Think about a time when something didn't work out as planned. Like Marcus's volcano, it might have seemed catastrophic in the moment. Write down:

- What happened?
- How did it feel?
- What was your first reaction?

Step 2: Finding Your Way Through

Consider your response:

- What strategies helped you cope?
- Who or what supported you?
- What self-talk helped you persist?

Step 3: Learning and Growing

Examine the experience through a growth mindset lens:

- What did you learn?
- How did it strengthen you?
- What wisdom emerged?

Step 4: Connecting to Your Child

Bridge your experience to your child's challenges:

- How might your story help them?
- What strategies could you share?
- How can your experience inform your support?

This reflection process helps us become more intentional in our parenting, turning our own setbacks into teaching tools. Just as Marcus transformed his collapsed volcano into a learning opportunity, we can help our children view challenges as stepping stones to growth.

The key is consistency by weaving these practices into daily life rather than reserving them for crises. Make emotional check-ins part of your routine, celebrate effort alongside achievement, and share your own growth stories. Remember, building resilience is like tending a garden—it requires patience, regular attention, and trust in the process of growth.

The Scientist's Challenge: Turning "Oops" Into "Aha!"

This activity can help children develop emotional resilience and a growth mindset.

What you'll need:

- your favorite building materials (LEGOs, blocks, paper, clay—anything you like!)
- a notebook and pencil
- timer (optional)
- a friend or family member (optional)

The mission: Just like Marcus with his volcano, you're going to be a scientist on a special mission! The twist is that instead of trying to make everything perfect, we're going to practice turning mistakes into discoveries.

Step 1: The Building Challenge (15 minutes)

- Choose something fun to build (a tower, a bridge, an animal—whatever you like!).
- Here's the important part: You have to make at least three "mistakes" while building.
- Each time something doesn't work, use your "Pause and Plan" power:
  - Take a deep breath and count to five.
  - Ask yourself: "What would a scientist do?"
  - Try a new way to solve the problem.

Step 2: Your Discovery Journal

For each "mistake," write down:

- What happened? (Example: "My tower fell over".)
- How did it feel? (Draw a weather symbol for your emotions!)
- What did you learn? (Example: "I needed a wider base".)
- What did you try next? (Example: "I made the bottom bigger".)

Step 3: Superhero Power-Up!

When you feel frustrated:

1. Strike your favorite superhero pose.
2. Take three big "superhero breaths".
3. Say your scientist power phrase: "Mistakes help me learn!"

Step 4: Share Your Story

Tell someone about

- your favorite "mistake" and what you learned
- what surprised you
- what you're proud of trying

Bonus challenge: Create a "Scientific Discoveries" wall or board where you can collect stories of times when mistakes led to something awesome.

Real scientists make their best discoveries by learning from the mistakes they made. Each time something doesn't work, you're not failing but collecting data for your next amazing idea.

From Classroom to Living Room: Resilience in Everyday Moments

The journey of building resilience doesn't just happen during science projects or formal activities. It can happen during small moments throughout our daily lives and even often when we least expect it.

Take the Thompson family's dinner preparation disaster. Ten-year-old Elle was determined to surprise her parents by making pasta sauce from scratch. She carefully followed the recipe her grandmother had taught her, measuring ingredients and stirring with concentration. When she reached for the oregano, the entire container tipped into the pot, turning her sauce into an herb-filled soup.

"My first thought was 'I ruined everything,'" Elle recalls. "But then I heard Ms. Rodriguez's voice in my head asking 'What would a scientist do?'"

Instead of dissolving into tears, Elle approached the problem methodically. She scooped out what herbs she could, added more tomatoes to dilute the flavor, and discovered that a bit of sugar helped balance the intensity. The resulting sauce wasn't exactly what she'd planned, but it was edible and came with a side of pride that tasted even better than the original recipe might have.

"What impressed me wasn't that she fixed the sauce," her father shared. "It was watching her work through that moment of panic and find her way to a solution. That skill matters more than perfect pasta."

Small Setbacks, Big Opportunities

These everyday challenges, spilled milk, lost homework, disagreements with friends might seem trivial compared to life's bigger hurdles. Yet, they provide the perfect training ground for building resilience muscles that will serve children throughout their lives.

Michael and David Kim witnessed this when their six-year-old daughter Mina struggled with a friendship conflict at school. After being excluded from a game at recess, Mina came home devastated.

"We almost called the other child's parents immediately," admits Michael. "But we remembered what we learned about helping kids develop their own problem-solving skills. So, instead, we used the weather report method, Mina said her feelings were 'thunderstorms with lightning', and then helped her brainstorm what she might say to her friend the next day."

The following afternoon, Mina proudly reported that she'd used her "brave words" to tell her friend how she felt, and they'd worked out a plan for including everyone. A small victory, perhaps, but one that built her confidence in navigating social challenges.

Celebrating Growth, Not Just Success

Perhaps most importantly, families that nurture resilience celebrate the journey, not just the destination. They notice and acknowledge

- when a child tries a new approach to a problem
- the moment a child pauses before reacting
- when siblings work through a conflict without adult intervention
- the courage to attempt something challenging, regardless of outcome

These celebrations don't require elaborate praise or rewards. Sometimes it's as simple as saying, "I noticed how you kept trying different ways to make that work. That kind of thinking will help you solve many problems in life."

As parents, teachers, and caregivers, we can't prevent children from experiencing setbacks and disappointments. Nor should we want to—these challenges are the very soil in which resilience grows. What we can do is provide the tools, support, and mindset that help them transform these moments from discouragements into building blocks for lifelong resilience.

The greatest gift of resilience is that it gives our children the ability to solve today's problems, and the confidence to deal with what tomorrow might bring.

Key Takeaways

- ❏ Building resilience in children involves teaching techniques like "Pause and Plan" or the "Weather Report Method" that help them navigate frustration and recognize emotions as temporary states that can be managed.
- ❏ Neuroplasticity principles show that each challenge creates an opportunity for developing stronger neural pathways, making emotional regulation skills more effective with consistent practice and repetition.
- ❏ Fostering a growth mindset transforms how children approach setbacks like Marcus reframing his collapsed volcano as a puzzle to solve rather than a failure—by replacing "I can't" with "I can't yet" and celebrating effort over outcomes.
- ❏ Everyday challenges provide perfect training grounds for resilience, as parents can use small setbacks as opportunities to help children develop problem-solving skills while celebrating the process of growth rather than just successful outcomes.

Chapter Three

EMOTIONAL INTELLIGENCE FOR IMPROVED CONNECTIONS

Alex sat in his car outside his daughter's elementary school, replaying the morning's events in his mind. Seven-year-old Sophie had thrown an impressive tantrum over mismatched socks, and his initial reaction had been frustration and impatience. However, then he remembered what he'd learned about emotional intelligence, and something clicked.

Instead of dismissing her feelings or rushing to fix the problem, he'd paused and really looked at his daughter's face. Behind the tears over seemingly trivial socks, he recognized the same anxious expression she'd worn since starting second grade with a new teacher. "You're feeling worried about a lot of things today, aren't you?" he'd asked softly. Sophie's sobs had quieted as she nodded, and what followed was a conversation about feeling out of control and scared of making mistakes in front of her classmates.

Now, watching Sophie confidently walk into school, mismatched socks and all, Alex smiled. That small moment of connection had transformed what could have been a disastrous morning into something meaningful. It wasn't about the socks at all; it never really was. By tuning into both his own emotions and his daughter's underlying feelings, he'd managed to turn a potential meltdown into a moment of understanding and growth.

Breaking Down Emotional Intelligence Into Actionable Skills

Alex's interaction with Sophie demonstrates emotional intelligence (EQ) in action—the ability to recognize, understand, and respond effectively to emotions in ourselves and others. Like Alex discovering the real story behind Sophie's sock tantrum, emotional intelligence helps us decode the deeper meanings behind behaviors and connect more meaningfully with our children.

Let's break down the five core components of emotional intelligence and explore how they manifest in daily parenting:

1. **Self-awareness:** Just as Alex recognized his initial frustration before choosing a different response, we can help children become emotional detectives of their own feelings.
    - **Practice:** During bedtime stories, ask "How do you think Goldilocks felt when she found the bears' house?" Then connect it to their experiences: "Have you ever felt nervous in a new place like that?"
2. **Self-regulation:** Alex modeled this by pausing to manage his frustration, showing Sophie that emotions can be navigated rather than controlled by them.
    - **Practice:** Create a "Calm Corner" with soft pillows and comfort items where children can practice self-regulation strategies.
    - **Model the behavior:** "I'm feeling frustrated right now, so I'm going to take three deep breaths to help me think clearly."
3. **Motivation:** This involves helping children develop internal drive and resilience, much like Sophie finding the courage to walk into school despite her anxieties.
    - **Practice:** The "Best and Worst" dinner game, where family members share their daily highs and lows, helping children process challenges and celebrate successes.
4. **Empathy:** Alex demonstrated this by looking beyond Sophie's behavior to understand her underlying feelings.
    - **Practice:** When reading stories or discussing playground interactions, ask questions like "How do you think your friend felt when...?"
    - **Guide children to notice emotional cues in others:** "Did you see how your sister smiled when you shared your toys?"
5. **Social skills:** These develop naturally when children feel secure in expressing and understanding emotions.
    - **Practice:** Role-play common social scenarios during playtime.
    - Use everyday interactions as teaching moments for appropriate emotional expression.

Empathy and Regulation in Daily Life

The power of emotional intelligence becomes most apparent in regular family routines and rituals. Predictable moments whether it's Sunday pancake breakfasts or bedtime stories create safe spaces for emotional expression and learning. When children know they can count on these consistent connections, they're more likely to share their feelings and work through challenging emotions.

Consider how Alex and Sophie's morning routine could have gone differently without emotional intelligence:

- Without self-awareness, Alex might have remained frustrated and escalated the situation.
- Without empathy, Sophie's underlying anxieties would have stayed hidden.
- Without self-regulation tools, both might have started their day in emotional turmoil.

Instead, their interaction showcases how emotional intelligence transforms everyday moments:

- Recognition: Alex noticed both his own frustration and Sophie's anxiety
- Understanding: He connected Sophie's behavior to her deeper feelings.
- Response: He chose to engage with empathy rather than frustration.
- Growth: Both parent and child learned from the experience.

To build these skills in your own family:

- Create daily check-in routines, like sharing "rose and thorn" moments at dinner.
- Establish predictable connection times where emotions can be safely explored.
- Validate feelings before moving to solutions: "That must feel really frustrating" instead of "You're fine".
- Use everyday challenges as opportunities to practice emotional skills together.

Remember, just as Sophie's mismatched socks became a bridge to deeper understanding, every challenging moment contains the potential for emotional growth and connection. The key isn't to avoid difficult feelings but to create an environment where all emotions are acknowledged, understood, and worked through together.

DAILY FAMILY RESILIENCE TRACKER

Today's Date: _____

Emotional Check-In

How are we feeling today? Complete this activity on a piece of paper. Draw or write your emotion.

- Parent: _____
- Child: _____

Today's Win

Share one moment where you handled a tricky situation well:

_____
_____

What helped you get through it?

_____
_____

Family Connection Moment

When did we connect today?

- What happened?
  _____

- How did we handle it?
  _____

- What did we learn?
  _____

Our Family Habits

✓ Check what we did today:

  ☐ shared a meal
  ☐ had a calm conversation about feelings

- ☐ practiced taking deep breaths when upset
- ☐ used "I feel…" statements
- ☐ created a safe space for emotions
- ☐ showed understanding when someone was upset

Tomorrow's Plan

One thing we want to try tomorrow to build our resilience:

Weekly Reflection

Look back at your daily trackers each weekend. What patterns do you notice?

What worked well?

_____
_____

What could we try differently?

_____
_____

What new family ritual could we start?

_____
_____

Example Entry

Date: January 10, 2025

Emotional check-In:

- Parent: Tired but proud
- Child: Nervous then brave

Today's win: Sophie was worried about mismatched socks, but we turned it into a conversation about feeling scared of mistakes at school. Instead of rushing to fix the socks, we talked about her feelings.

Family connection moment:

- ❑ **What happened?** Sophie had anxiety about school.
- ❑ **How did we handle it?** I stopped to listen instead of dismiss.
- ❑ **What we learned?** Sometimes little problems show bigger feelings.

Family habits today:

✓ had calm conversation about feelings

✓ created safe space for emotions

✓ showed understanding when upset

Tomorrow's plan: Start the day with a quick check-in about how we're feeling before school.

Key Takeaways

- ❑ Emotional intelligence in parenting involves looking beyond a child's behavior to understand the underlying feelings.
- ❑ The five core components of emotional intelligence—self-awareness, self-regulation, motivation, empathy, and social skills—can be developed through daily practices like emotion check-ins, modeling calm responses, and validating feelings before offering solutions.
- ❑ Consistent family routines and predictable connection times create safe spaces for emotional expression, making children more likely to share their feelings and work through challenging emotions.
- ❑ Every challenging moment contains potential for emotional growth and connection when parents use self-awareness to manage their own reactions and respond with empathy rather than frustration.

Chapter Four

MINDFUL PARENTING AND BREAKING GENERATIONAL PATTERNS

Maria caught herself mid-sentence, her mother's words echoing in her own voice: "Because I said so!" The phrase hung in the air between her and her six-year-old son, Jake, who stood defiantly beside his untouched vegetables. She felt that familiar tightness in her chest—the same tension she'd experienced as a child when those words were directed at her.

Taking a deep breath, she closed her eyes for a moment. This wasn't the parent she wanted to be. Her own mother had ruled with an iron fist of absolutes and unquestionable authority, leaving little room for discussion or understanding. Now here she was, unconsciously following the same script.

"Let's try this again," Maria said softly, pulling out a chair and patting the seat next to her. Jake approached cautiously, surprise replacing his defensive stance. "Can you tell me why you don't want to eat your vegetables today?"

As Jake opened up about how the broccoli reminded him of the "yucky" cafeteria food that made him feel sick last week, Maria realized something profound. This moment—this simple conversation about vegetables—wasn't just about dinner. It was about breaking a chain, about writing a new story for both of them.

Each time she chose understanding over authority, patience over power, she wasn't just parenting differently; she was healing her own inner child too.

Understanding Polyvagal Theory and Its Application in Parenting

Maria's interaction with Jake illustrates polyvagal theory in action—the intricate connection between our nervous system and our emotional responses. Just as Maria noticed her physical tension and consciously chose to shift her approach, our bodies constantly navigate between different nervous system states that influence our reactions and relationships.

Think of your nervous system as having three primary "modes," each serving a distinct purpose. Understanding these modes helps us recognize and respond to our children's emotional states more effectively.

The first mode is the sympathetic state, often called our "fight or flight" response. This is what we saw in Maria's initial tension and Jake's defiance. When activated, it shows up as heightened energy, defensiveness, or anxiety. You might notice physical signs like rapid heartbeat, shallow breathing, and muscle tension.

The second mode is the parasympathetic state, our "rest and restore" system. This is what Maria accessed when she took a deep breath and reset her approach. This state enables calm, thoughtful responses and is characterized by slower breathing, relaxed muscles, and clearer thinking.

The third mode is the social engagement system, which Maria and Jake reached during their conversation. This state facilitates connection, understanding, and problem-solving. It's marked by open communication, engaged facial expressions, and emotional attunement.

When we understand these states, we can respond more effectively to our children's needs. For instance, when we see a child in fight/flight mode (like Jake's initial defiance), we can use specific strategies to help them shift toward safety and connection.

Creating physical and emotional safety becomes key. This might mean using a gentle voice and open posture. We can offer co-regulation through our calm presence and deep breathing. Face-to-face connection and warm expressions signal safety to our child's nervous system.

Techniques for Self-Regulation and Reframing Negative Self-Talk

Maria's story demonstrates how self-awareness can interrupt generational patterns. When she caught herself repeating her mother's words, she employed key self-regulation techniques that we can all learn from.

The first step is recognition—noticing those physical sensations of tension or stress in our bodies. Maria felt it as tightness in her chest. For others, it might be a clenched jaw, tight shoulders, or shallow breathing.

Next comes the pause—that crucial moment of taking a breath to create space for choice. This pause doesn't need to be long; even a few seconds can be enough to interrupt automatic responses.

The final step is reset—consciously choosing a different approach aligned with our values. For Maria, this meant shifting from authority to understanding, from power to connection.

To develop these skills in your own parenting journey, start with regular body awareness practices. Notice your physical tension signals throughout the day. Try to identify emotional triggers before they escalate. Make a habit of checking in with yourself during routine moments, like washing dishes or driving.

Challenging negative self-talk becomes easier with practice. When you hear that inner voice saying "I'm failing as a parent," practice reframing it as "I'm learning and growing." Replace "I should know better" with "I'm discovering better ways." Transform "I'm just like my mother/father" into "I can choose my own parenting path."

Creating a Consistent and Safe Emotional Environment

The transformation in Maria and Jake's interaction shows how a safe emotional environment enables authentic connection. Like Maria creating space for Jake to express his true feelings about the vegetables, we can build trust through consistent practices.

Daily rituals become the foundation of emotional safety. These might include regular check-in conversations during dinner or bedtime. Setting aside designated time for undivided attention shows your child they matter. Responding consistently to emotional needs builds trust over time.

Physical and emotional safety cues play a crucial role. Using a calm voice and maintaining open body language helps children feel secure. Practicing active listening without judgment encourages them to share more openly. Establishing predictable routines and boundaries provides the structure children need to feel safe.

Remember Maria's realization: It's not just about the vegetables, or the tantrums, or the defiance. Each interaction is an opportunity to break old patterns and create new ones.

By understanding our nervous system states, practicing self-regulation, and maintaining a consistent emotional environment, we create spaces where both parents and children can grow, heal, and thrive together. Every small moment of connection, every conscious choice to respond differently, contributes to this transformation.

Parent's Guide: Handling Tough Moments

Daily Conversation Starters

Instead of "How was your day?" try:

- "What made you laugh today?"
- "Did anything surprise you at school?"
- "Who did you play with at recess?"

Common Scenarios and Response Scripts

BULLYING AT SCHOOL

Scenario: Your child tells you someone made fun of their lunch or clothes.

Instead of: "Just ignore them" or "Don't let it bother you".

Try this approach:

- First response: "That must have felt really uncomfortable. Do you want to tell me more about what happened?"
- Listen fully, then: "How did that make you feel?"
- Problem solve together: "What do you think you'd like to do if this happens again? We can come up with some ideas together."
- Offer specific strategies: "Would you like to practice some ways to respond? We could try saying 'I don't like that' in a strong voice."

FRIENDSHIP TROUBLES

Scenario: Your child wasn't invited to a classmate's party.

Instead of: "It's not a big deal" or "We'll have our own party".

Try this:

- ❏ **Acknowledge**: "It can really hurt when you're left out. I remember feeling that way too."
- ❏ **Listen**: "Would you like to talk about how you're feeling?"
- ❏ **Support**: "You're a great friend, and this doesn't change that."
- ❏ **Plan**: "Should we plan something fun this weekend? Maybe invite Sarah over?"

Key Takeaways

- ❏ Breaking generational parenting patterns requires self-awareness.
- ❏ Polyvagal theory explains how our nervous system operates in three primary modes—the fight/flight sympathetic state, the rest/restore parasympathetic state, and the connection-oriented social engagement system—which directly influence our parenting responses.
- ❏ Effective self-regulation involves recognizing physical tension signals, pausing to create space for choice, and consciously resetting to align with our parenting values rather than automatic reactions.
- ❏ Creating emotional safety through consistent routines, active listening, and specific communication techniques transforms difficult moments into opportunities for connection, helping both parents and children develop healthier relationship patterns.

Chapter Five

THE COMPLETE PARENT'S TOOLKIT FOR RAISING SOCIALLY THRIVING KIDS

Seven-year-old Nicole stood at the edge of the playground, clutching her favorite stuffed penguin. It was her first day at a new school, and the swirling energy of laughing children and rapid-fire conversations felt overwhelming. Then she noticed a small group of kids building what looked like a city in the sandbox. One girl was frowning at a collapsed tower, while another was excitedly gesturing toward the sky, probably sharing grand architectural plans.

Gathering her courage, Nicole approached the sandbox. "Maybe if you pat the sand more firmly, the tower won't fall," she suggested quietly. The girl with the fallen tower looked up, surprise turning to interest. Soon, Nicole found herself kneeling in the sand beside Zara and Jin, their architectural ambitions growing with each handful of sand. Together, they built not just a sandcastle, but the foundation of new friendships—each child contributing their unique strengths while learning to connect with others.

Developing Social Intelligence and Adaptability

Nicole's sandbox interaction demonstrates how children naturally develop social skills through everyday experiences. Like a toolbox that gradually fills with useful instruments, children acquire and refine their social abilities through each interaction. Nicole's observation of body language—noting the frustrated frown over the collapsed tower—and her thoughtful approach to offering help showcases key elements of social intelligence in action.

Children instinctively pick up on non-verbal cues, but we can help them develop this awareness more consciously. Teaching them to notice and interpret social signals enriches their interactions:

- A friend's slumped shoulders during recess might signal a need for support.
- An excited bounce often indicates enthusiasm and readiness to play.
- Crossed arms and turned away faces could suggest discomfort or disagreement.

This awareness becomes particularly valuable when joining established groups, like Nicole approaching the sandbox builders. Children learn to read the social atmosphere and find appropriate ways to participate. They discover how to

- observe group dynamics before joining in.
- offer relevant contributions (like Nicole's building suggestion).
- balance self-expression with group cooperation.

Strategies for Confident and Authentic Relationship-Building

Building on these foundational social awareness skills, children can develop more sophisticated strategies for forming genuine connections. Consider how Nicole's approach to the sandbox group exemplified several key principles:

Self-expression:

- She shared her knowledge about building sandcastles.
- Her suggestion was offered gently, respecting the existing group dynamic.
- She remained authentic to herself while adapting to the group.

Creating opportunities for self-expression at home helps children practice these skills in a safe environment:

- Set up creative spaces where children can freely share ideas.
- Encourage various forms of expression (art, storytelling, movement).
- Validate their thoughts and feelings while guiding appropriate expression.

Role-playing builds confidence for real-world interactions:

- Practice common social scenarios through imaginative play.
- Explore different responses to challenging situations.
- Build adaptability by trying various social roles.

Active listening strengthens connections:

- Make eye contact to show engagement.
- Ask follow-up questions about others' ideas.
- Show genuine interest in different perspectives.

Fostering Resilience Through Empathy

The sandbox scene also illustrates how empathy and perspective-taking develop through real interactions. Nicole's ability to recognize Zara's frustration with the collapsed tower and offer helpful suggestions demonstrates emerging empathy skills.

To nurture these capabilities:

Create "Empathy Moments" in daily life:

- Notice others' emotional states.
- Discuss possible reasons for those feelings.
- Brainstorm ways to help or respond.
- Take action when appropriate.
- Reflect on the outcomes.

Practice perspective-taking through regular activities:

- During story time, pause to explore characters' feelings.
- At dinner, share daily challenges and discuss different viewpoints.
- In conflicts, help children consider all perspectives involved.

Track progress through reflection:

- "Remember when you helped with the fallen tower? How did that make you feel?"
- "What did you learn from playing with new friends today?"
- "How might we handle a similar situation next time?"

Just as Nicole's sandbox experience grew from a simple building suggestion into collaborative play and friendship, each social interaction offers opportunities for growth. By helping children understand and practice these skills, we equip them to build meaningful connections while staying true to themselves.

The key is making these practices part of daily life rather than formal lessons. Whether it's joining a playground game, sharing toys, or working through disagreements, every interaction becomes a chance to develop social intelligence, empathy, and resilience.

Interactive Social Skills Exercise: The Friendship Garden

This exercise helps children practice social awareness, empathy, and relationship-building skills through a guided group activity. It builds on the natural way children learn through play while incorporating the key principles discussed in the text.

Setup

- time required: 30-45 minutes
- age range: 6-8 years old
- group size: 4-6 children
- materials needed
    - large paper or poster board
    - colored markers or crayons
    - craft materials (optional: stickers, glitter, construction paper)
    - "seed cards" (index cards with different social scenarios written on them)

THE ACTIVITY: GROWING OUR FRIENDSHIP GARDEN

Part 1: Planning the Garden (10 minutes)

Each child receives a section of the large paper to create their own garden plot. Before they start drawing, facilitate a group discussion:

- What does your garden need to grow? (Like friendships need care and attention).
- How will you make space for other plants? (Like making space for new friends).
- What makes your garden special? (Like what makes each person unique).

Part 2: Planting Seeds of Friendship (15 minutes)

Children take turns drawing "seed cards" with scenarios like:

- "A new student looks lonely during recess."

- "Someone's art project gets accidentally damaged."
- "Two friends both want to use the same swing."
- "Someone is having trouble with a math problem."

For each scenario, the group

- identifies the feelings involved (practicing empathy).
- brainstorms helpful responses (developing social strategies).
- adds a flower, plant, or garden element to their section representing how they would handle the situation.
- explains their drawing to the group (practicing self-expression).

Part 3: Growing Together (10 minutes)

Children connect their individual garden plots by:

- drawing paths between gardens (representing ways to connect with others).
- adding elements that span multiple sections (showing cooperation).
- creating a garden feature together (practicing group work).

Part 4: Reflection (5-10 minutes)

Guide a group discussion using questions like:

- How did it feel to share your garden ideas with others?
- What was challenging about working together?
- What new things did you learn about your classmates?
- How can we use these ideas on the playground?

Assessment Opportunities

Observe children's:

- ability to identify emotions in scenarios
- willingness to consider multiple perspectives
- cooperation in group elements
- communication of ideas and feelings
- creative problem-solving approaches

Tips for Facilitators

- Validate all appropriate solutions; there are many ways to handle social situations.
- Encourage children to build on each other's ideas.
- Use gentle prompts to help quiet children contribute.
- Connect the activity to real playground and classroom situations.
- Celebrate examples of children using these skills in daily life.

Follow-Up

- Reference the friendship garden when helping children navigate real social situations.
- Add new elements to the garden as children develop new social skills.
- Share the garden concept with families to reinforce skills at home.
- Use the garden metaphor in future discussions about friendship and social growth.

Key Takeaways

- ❑ Children develop social intelligence through natural interactions.
- ❑ Building authentic relationships involves balancing self-expression with group cooperation, requiring skills in active listening, reading non-verbal cues, and adapting to social situations while remaining true to oneself.
- ❑ Empathy and perspective-taking are critical social skills that can be fostered through "Empathy Moments" in daily life, where children learn to notice others' emotions, consider reasons for those feelings, and take appropriate actions to help.
- ❑ Social skills development works best when integrated into everyday activities and play rather than formal lessons, allowing children to practice these abilities in authentic situations with guided reflection afterward.

Conclusion

Let's talk about this amazing journey we're all on as parents. You know those days when everything goes perfectly; your kid shares their toys without being asked, handles a disappointment with grace, or shows kindness to a friend? And then there are those other days... when the wrong color cup leads to a meltdown of epic proportions! That's parenting for you. It can be a wild mix of proud moments and "What do I do now?" situations.

Think about the last time you felt really overwhelmed. Maybe it was a tough day at work or a stressful situation with a friend. Chances are, you had someone to turn to who would listen without judgment and help you feel better. That's exactly what our kids need from us. When your child knows they can come to you with anything, they develop the confidence to face life's challenges. This shows up in small ways every day, like when your first-grader comes home upset because no one would play with them at recess. Instead of jumping in with solutions, you listen, give them a hug, and help them think through what they might try tomorrow. These moments might seem small, but they're actually building your child's emotional foundation.

Remember that math homework meltdown? We've all been there! Instead of saying "It's not that hard" (even though we might want to), try sitting down and saying, "This looks tricky. Let's break it down together." When we help kids see challenges as puzzles to solve rather than insurmountable obstacles, something magical happens. They start developing problem-solving skills that will serve them well throughout their lives. These small shifts in how we approach difficulties can transform frustrating moments into opportunities for growth.

Watch a group of kids at play, and you'll see emotional intelligence in action. Maybe your child notices a friend looking left out and invites them to join the game. Or perhaps they take a deep breath to calm down instead of lashing out when someone cuts in line. These moments show that our kids are learning to understand and manage both their own feelings and those of others. It's like watching tiny seeds of empathy and self-regulation bloom into beautiful flowers.

Let's be honest. We all have days when we don't handle things as well as we'd like. Maybe you lost your cool during the morning rush, or didn't respond as patiently as you wanted to that hundredth "why?" question. Here's the beautiful truth: These imperfect moments are actually opportunities to model resilience and honesty. When we apologize to our kids and show them how to make things right, we're teaching valuable lessons about relationships and responsibility.

We're all familiar with those big feeling moments; the tears over a broken toy, the frustration of learning something new, the anxiety about a new situation. Picture this: Your four-year-old is having a complete meltdown in the grocery store because you won't buy their favorite cereal. Your face gets hot as other shoppers stare, and you're tempted to either give in or lose your cool. Then you remember that this is a chance to teach emotional regulation. You get down to their level, acknowledge their disappointment, and help them work through it. It's not always pretty, but these are the moments that shape our children's emotional development.

Looking ahead, we'll explore practical ways to help our kids navigate these emotional waters. We'll dive into strategies like creating a "calm down corner" where kids can go to process big feelings, using fun games to help them identify and express their emotions, and finding ways to stay calm ourselves when our kids are struggling. These tools aren't just nice-to-have extras. They're essential skills that will help our children navigate relationships, handle stress, and build resilience throughout their lives.

Remember, raising emotionally strong kids isn't about having all the answers or never making mistakes. It's about being there consistently for our kids, helping them understand and manage their feelings, teaching them that challenges are opportunities to grow, and showing them that it's okay to make mistakes and try again. By showing up each day, trying your best, and loving your kids through both the smooth and bumpy patches, you're already giving them what they need most, namely a secure foundation from which to grow into emotionally strong individuals.

If you managed to get through today without any major meltdowns (yours or theirs), consider it a win, otherwise you can try again tomorrow. That's the beautiful thing about this parenting journey, each day brings new opportunities to learn and grow together. As we move forward, remember that you're not alone in this adventure. Every parent has days when they wonder if they're doing it right, but it's the consistent love and support we provide that matters most in the end.

Book Three

Introduction

Remember the last time your child melted down in the grocery store? Or maybe it was at bedtime, when they suddenly couldn't bear to wear the pajamas they loved yesterday? In these moments, it's easy to feel overwhelmed and wonder, "Why didn't anyone teach me how to handle this?" While most of us can recall learning algebra or world history, few of us received any guidance on understanding emotions—our own or our children's.

What we're really talking about is emotional intelligence not just managing tantrums, but building a foundation for lifelong emotional well-being. Research shows that children who develop strong emotional intelligence tend to form better relationships, handle stress more effectively, and even perform better academically. The good news? These skills can be taught and strengthened over time.

Let's look at this through a practical lens. When your child refuses to wear those previously-loved pajamas, they might be expressing something deeper—perhaps feeling overwhelmed by their day or needing more control in their environment. Instead of rushing to fix the situation, try this approach:

- Pause and observe: Notice their body language and tone.
- Validate their experience: "It seems like you're really frustrated right now".
- Get curious: "Can you tell me more about what's bothering you?"

This simple shift from problem-solving to understanding can transform these challenging moments into opportunities for emotional growth. Take Sarah's experience with her four-year-old Jake: "Instead of panicking during meltdowns, I learned to say, 'You seem really upset. Can you tell me more?' Just showing I wanted to understand helped him calm down faster."

Creating an emotionally intelligent home doesn't mean emotions run wild - it's about finding balance. When your six-year-old gets angry about sharing toys, acknowledge the feeling while setting clear boundaries: "It's okay to feel angry, but we don't hit. Let's find another way to handle these big feelings."

Reflection points:

- How did your family handle emotions when you were growing up?
- What patterns do you notice in your child's emotional responses?
- Which situations consistently trigger emotional overwhelm for your child?

Remember, you're modeling emotional intelligence every day. Share your own experiences: "Mommy felt frustrated at work today, so I took some deep breaths and found a solution." These real-life examples show children that everyone has big feelings and there are healthy ways to manage them.

Start with these simple daily practices:

- Emotion check-ins at dinner: "What made you happy/sad today?"
- Create a calming corner with soft items and quiet activities
- Name emotions as they happen: "You're jumping - you must be excited!"

Your journey in emotional intelligence parenting won't be perfect, and that's okay. Use challenging moments to model emotional repair: "I'm sorry I yelled. I was overwhelmed, but that's not a good reason to raise my voice. Can we try again?"

Next step challenge: This week, focus on emotion labeling. Notice and name three emotions your child experiences each day, helping them build their emotional vocabulary while strengthening your connection.

Remember: Each time you validate a feeling or help your child find words for their emotions, you're building skills that will serve them throughout their lives. Start small, stay consistent, and watch emotional intelligence grow in your home.

Chapter One

WHAT IS EMOTIONAL INTELLIGENCE?

My six-year-old daughter came home from school last week, slammed her backpack down, and burst into tears. Not the usual "I had a bad day" tears, but the kind that made me stop everything and sit with her. Turns out, her best friend had played with someone else at recess. "She doesn't like me anymore," she sobbed.

Instead of jumping in with "she's still your friend" or "you'll find other friends," I just sat there and asked, "That must have felt really lonely today, huh?"

Her eyes got wide, like she was surprised I understood. We talked about all the feelings swirling around inside her—the sadness, the jealousy, even a little anger. Then she said something that amazed me: "Maybe Sarah wanted to play with Amy because she never gets to play with her. I sometimes feel sad when I don't get to play with other friends too."

Just like that, my little girl had shown more emotional intelligence than I probably had at twice her age. She went from feeling rejected to understanding someone else's perspective, all because we took the time to talk about her big feelings, instead of rushing to fix them.

The Five Pillars of Emotional Intelligence

Think of emotional intelligence as building blocks that help your child understand and manage their feelings. While we'll explore these concepts throughout different situations in later chapters, let's quickly break down the five key pillars that form the foundation of emotional intelligence.

Self-Awareness

This is your child's ability to recognize and name their emotions. Instead of just having a meltdown, they learn to say, "I'm frustrated because I can't make this puzzle work." It's like giving them an emotional vocabulary that grows with them.

Emotional Regulation

Once children can name their feelings, they need tools to manage them. Whether it's taking deep breaths during anger or finding a quiet spot when overwhelmed, these coping strategies become lifelong skills.

Motivation

This isn't about pushing for perfection—it's about developing resilience. When your child faces challenges, they learn to push through difficulties and understand that struggle is a normal part of growth.

Empathy

Understanding others' feelings helps children build stronger relationships. It's the difference between walking past a crying friend and stopping to ask what's wrong.

Social Skills

This final piece ties everything together. When children understand their own emotions and those of others, they're better equipped to navigate friendships, resolve conflicts, and communicate effectively.

These pillars work together to help your child develop emotional maturity. As we explore different parenting scenarios in the coming chapters, you'll see how these foundations naturally weave into daily interactions with your child.

Determining Emotional Intelligence

Maybe you're wondering how emotionally smart your child really is, and if it can be measured. Just like we can track how tall they're growing, we can actually get a sense of how they're developing emotionally.

An emotional intelligence quiz can give you an understanding of where your child is right now and where they might need a little extra support. Maybe they're amazing at knowing how they feel, but struggle to understand why their little sister is crying. That's totally normal, and now you know exactly what to work on.

The results of the quiz can help you start conversations that matter. When you ask your kid "How do you feel when you make a mistake?" or "What do you do when you're really angry?" you're not just collecting answers—you're opening doors to talk about stuff that really matters.

Let's say the quiz shows your child has a hard time calming down when upset. Instead of just knowing this, you can work together to find solutions. Maybe they discover that counting to ten actually helps, or that drawing their feelings works better than trying to explain them. These become their personal tools for handling big emotions.

The real magic happens when these conversations become part of everyday life. It could be as simple as asking "How do you think your friend felt when that happened?" during dinner, or practicing deep breaths together before a challenging situation.

Remember, this isn't about turning your kid into an emotional genius overnight. It's about growing together, celebrating small wins (like the first time they calm themselves down without help), and building skills that'll serve them well beyond the playground years.

Social Skills

While academic skills are important, kids also need to become socially savvy.

Think about your child's day. They're constantly navigating social situations, from figuring out whom to sit with at lunch to working on group projects or joining a new after-school club. These moments might seem small, but they're actually huge opportunities for growth. It's in these everyday interactions that kids learn the art of getting along with others.

The cool thing is, strong social skills naturally boost confidence. Watch a kid who's comfortable talking to others, who knows how to join a game at recess, or who can work through a disagreement with a friend - they tend to be happier and more relaxed. They're not born with these skills; they're learning them, one interaction at a time.

So, how do we help? It's simpler than you might think. When your kid comes home upset about playground drama, resist the urge to jump in with solutions. Instead, ask questions that help them think it through: "How do you think your friend felt when that happened?" or "What could you try next time?" These conversations can teach them empathy and problem-solving all at once.

Set up opportunities for practice too. Playdates, sports teams, or even family game nights are perfect training grounds for taking turns, reading body language, and dealing with wins and losses gracefully. Don't forget that you're children are watching you. When they see you navigate your social world with kindness and respect, they're picking up tips for their own interactions.

Child's Emotional Intelligence Quiz

For Children Ages 6-12

Read each scenario and question to your child. Help them choose the answer that best matches how they usually feel or act. Remember to emphasize that there are no "wrong" answers—this quiz helps understand their emotional world better.

SELF-AWARENESS SECTION

When something upsets you, do you:

Scenario: Imagine you're building with blocks and your tower keeps falling down...

1. Know exactly what you're feeling ("I feel frustrated because my tower won't stay up").
2. Feel mixed up inside but can't explain why (You know you feel bad but aren't sure why).
3. Not think about the feeling (Just keep building or walk away).
4. Get angry without knowing why (Knock all the blocks down).

If you make a mistake, how do you usually feel?

Scenario: During art class, you accidentally spill paint on your drawing...

1. It's okay, everyone makes mistakes ("I can try to make it into something new!") Really upset but can talk about it ("I'm sad but I can start over").
2. Want to hide it (Try to cover up the spill and hope no one notices).
3. Get mad at yourself (Crumple up the paper and refuse to try again).

When you're happy, can you tell why you're feeling that way?

Scenario: You're smiling and feeling great during recess...

    1. Yes, always ("I'm happy because I'm playing my favorite game with my friends").
    2. Usually ("I think it's because we're playing together").
    3. Sometimes (You're smiling but not sure why).
    4. Not really (You just know you feel good).

EMOTIONAL REGULATION SECTION

When something makes you really angry, what do you usually do?

Scenario: Someone cuts in front of you in the lunch line, you...

    1. Take deep breaths and try to calm down (Count to 10 quietly).
    2. Talk to someone about it (Tell a teacher how you feel).
    3. Yell or cry ("Hey, that's not fair!").
    4. Break things or hit something (Push the person or stomp your feet).

If you're feeling nervous about something, what helps you feel better?

Scenario: Tomorrow is your turn to present your show-and-tell item...

    1. Talking to someone you trust (Tell your parents why you're worried).
    2. Taking deep breaths (Practice breathing like smelling flowers and blowing bubbles).
    3. Trying to ignore the feeling (Go play and pretend it's not happening).
    4. Nothing helps (Worry all night and can't sleep).

EMPATHY SECTION

When your friend is sad, what do you do?

Scenario: Your friend's pet fish died...

    1. Try to understand why and help them feel better ("I know you loved your fish. Want to draw a picture of it?").
    2. Feel sad too but don't know what to do (Sit quietly with them).

3. Try to cheer them up right away ("Let's go play something fun!").
4. Leave them alone (Walk away and play with someone else).

If someone in your class is having a hard time with schoolwork, how do you feel?

Scenario: You notice your classmate can't solve the math problem everyone else finished...

1. Want to help them ("Would you like me to explain how I solved it?").
2. Feel bad for them (Look at them with concern but stay quiet).
3. Don't really notice (Keep working on your own work).
4. Think they should try harder ("It's so easy!").

SOCIAL SKILLS SECTION

When playing with others, do you:

Scenario: You're playing board games during indoor recess...

1. Share and take turns easily (Wait patiently for your turn).
2. Share but find it hard sometimes (Fidget while waiting but still wait).
3. Prefer to play by your own rules ("Let's skip that rule, it's boring").
4. Get upset if things don't go your way (Quit if you're losing).

If you disagree with a friend, what do you usually do?

Scenario: Your friend wants to play tag, but you want to play hide-and-seek...

1. Talk it out and try to understand each other ("We could play tag first, then hide-and-seek").
2. Go along with what they want (Play tag even though you don't want to).
3. Get upset but stay quiet (Play alone instead).
4. Argue until you win (Keep saying "No!" until they give in).

When working in a group, do you:

Scenario: Your class is working together to create a big art mural...

1. Listen to everyone's ideas ("What colors do you think we should use?").

2. Share your ideas but find it hard to listen (Keep talking about your ideas while others try to speak).
3. Let others do most of the talking (Stay quiet and just paint where told).
4. Want everything done your way ("My way will look better!").

SCORING GUIDE

Count how many of each letter your child chose:

- Mostly 1: strong emotional intelligence skills
- Mostly 2: developing emotional awareness
- Mostly 3: beginning to explore emotions
- Mostly 4: may need extra support with emotional skills

Next Steps and Activities

FOR SELF-AWARENESS (IF MOSTLY 3 OR 4):

- Create an "emotion words" wall at home.
  - Draw faces showing different emotions.
  - Write feeling words under each face.
  - Add new words as you learn them.
- Keep a feelings journal.
  - Draw a face showing how you feel each day.
  - Write or tell why you feel that way.
- Play "Emotion Detective".
  - Look at pictures in books or magazines.
  - Guess how the people are feeling.
  - Discuss what clues helped you guess.

FOR EMOTIONAL REGULATION (IF MOSTLY 3 OR 4):

- Practice "Balloon Breathing".
  - Pretend your belly is a balloon.
  - Breathe in to inflate it.
  - Breathe out to deflate it.

- Create a "Calm Down Corner".
    - Add soft pillows.
    - Include stress balls or fidget toys.
    - Put up pictures of peaceful places.
- Make a "Feel Better" toolbox.
    - Draw pictures of things that make you happy.
    - Include small toys that help you calm down.
    - Add photos of people who make you feel safe.

FOR EMPATHY (IF MOSTLY 3 OR 4):

- Read stories together.
    - Stop and discuss how characters might feel.
    - Ask "What would you do in their situation?"
    - Think about how different characters see the same event.
- Play "Feeling Mirror".
    - Take turns showing different emotions.
    - Other person copies and names the emotion.
    - Talk about times you've felt that way.
- Practice "Caring Cards".
    - Make cards for people who might need cheering up.
    - Write what you think might help them feel better.
    - Share times when others have helped you feel better.

FOR SOCIAL SKILLS (IF MOSTLY 3 OR 4):

- Play cooperative games.
    - Choose games where everyone works together.
    - Practice taking turns.
    - Celebrate team accomplishments.
- Practice "Good Listening".
    - Make eye contact.
    - Nod to show you're listening.
    - Ask questions about what the other person said.
- Role-play solving conflicts.
    - Act out common disagreements.
    - Practice using "I feel" statements.
    - Take turns suggesting solutions.

Emotional intelligence develops over time. Celebrate small improvements and make learning about emotions a regular part of your daily routine.

Try This Now

Start an "Emotions Check-In" at dinner tonight.

Ask each family member to share:

- one feeling they had today.
- what made them feel that way.

Keep it light and playful. There are no wrong answers! This simple five-minute activity helps children practice naming their emotions (self-awareness) while learning about others' feelings (empathy). Plus, it's a great way to start making emotional conversations part of your daily routine.

If your child says "good" or "bad," gently encourage them to be more specific: "What kind of good? Excited? Proud? Happy?"

Key Takeaways

- ❏ Emotional intelligence is built on five foundational pillars: self-awareness (recognizing and naming emotions), emotional regulation (managing feelings with appropriate tools), motivation (developing resilience), empathy (understanding others' perspectives), and social skills (navigating relationships effectively).
- ❏ Validating children's emotions before rushing to solutions creates space for them to process feelings and develop perspective, as shown when the mother simply acknowledged her daughter's loneliness about her friend playing with someone else.
- ❏ Social skills development happens through everyday interactions and conversations that encourage children to consider others' perspectives, with parents serving as models by navigating their own social world with kindness and respect.
- ❏ Regular emotional check-ins, like discussing feelings during family dinner or using an emotional intelligence quiz, help children build their emotional vocabulary and provide opportunities to practice identifying, discussing, and managing emotions in a supportive environment.

Chapter Two

BUILDING EMOTIONAL AWARENESS

Four-year-old Lucas sat hunched in the reading corner, his lower lip trembling after a chaotic playdate where his best friend had knocked down his carefully built tower. His dad, Thomas, found him there, clutching his worn superhero cape.

Rather than jumping to solutions, Thomas pulled out their special "emotion cards"—a tool that had become their secret language for tough moments. "Which one looks like you right now, buddy?" he asked gently. Lucas pointed to the "angry" face, then hesitantly touched the "disappointed" one, too.

"You know what?" Thomas said, settling beside him. "Sometimes big feelings come in pairs." Lucas nodded, then used the deep "dragon breaths" they'd practiced, breathing in through the nose, out through the mouth like a sleepy dragon. "I wanted to show Jack my tower," he explained, his voice steadier now. "But maybe... Maybe we can build an even bigger one together?"

Thomas smiled, as he watched his son transform a moment of frustration into an opportunity for connection.

Tools for Identifying and Expressing Emotions

Helping kids understand their feelings is like teaching them a new language, and visual tools can make this learning process more concrete and engaging. Emotion cards serve as feeling flashcards, displaying various facial expressions from joy to frustration. Make these cards accessible by placing them in frequently visited spots like the fridge or bedroom, then incorporate them into daily activities. Ask your child to match cards to their experiences: "Show me how you felt at today's playdate" or "Which face matches your feelings about the dentist visit?"

Pay attention to emotional triggers and patterns, such as anxiety before swimming lessons or frustration during toy-sharing. Use these observations to develop targeted coping strategies together. Establish regular feelings check-ins during natural daily transitions, like breakfast or bedtime, using simple prompts or visual aids such as a feeling's thermometer where children can indicate their emotional temperature.

The ultimate goal isn't to eliminate challenging emotions but to equip children with tools to recognize and manage their feelings effectively.

Techniques for Emotional Labeling and Trigger Recognition

Helping kids understand their feelings is almost like teaching them a new language. Just like we use picture books to teach words, we can use simple tools to help them name their emotions.

Emotion cards are like a deck of feeling flashcards. Each one shows a face expressing different emotions, from big smiles to frustrated frowns. Keep these cards handy, maybe on the fridge or in their room, and make it a game: "Pick a card that matches how you feel about today's playdate!" or "Which card shows how you felt when we went to the dentist?"

It's also helpful to notice what sets off big feelings. Maybe your child gets nervous before swimming lessons or upset when it's time to share toys. When you spot these patterns, you can work together on solutions, for example, like taking deep breaths before jumping in the pool or practicing sharing during playtime.

Try making feelings check-ins part of your daily routine, like during breakfast or before bed. It can be as simple as asking, "How's your heart feeling today?" Some families use a feeling's thermometer on the wall. Children can then move a marker to show if they're feeling "cool as a cucumber" or "hot and bothered."

Remember, the goal isn't to eliminate difficult emotions but to help kids recognize and handle them better. It's like giving them a toolbox for their feelings, one tool at a time.

The Feelings Time Capsule: Your Child's Emotional Journey Box

The Feelings Time Capsule: A Three-Step Guide to Emotional Learning

A simple activity to help children ages 4-10 understand their emotions.

Step 1: Create your feelings box (one-time setup)

- Let your child decorate a shoebox with their favorite colors, stickers, or drawings.
- Stock it with basic supplies: paper, crayons, a small notebook, and magazine photos showing different emotions.

Step 2: Daily emotion check-in (5-10 minutes)

- Have your child draw their current feeling (using faces, colors, or weather symbols).
- Let them match it with a photo from your collection.
- Ask them to place both in their box with a simple note about what caused the feeling.

Step 3: Weekly family review

- Spend time together looking through the week's collection.
- Discuss emotional patterns.
- Add new coping strategy cards to the "Solutions Corner" (like "Take deep breaths" or "Ask for hugs").

Keep the activity playful and child-led, celebrating all emotions as they build this valuable emotional toolkit.

Taking an Emotion Walk Together

Next time you're out with your child, turn your regular walk into a feelings-spotting adventure. It's as simple as noticing the world around you through an emotional lens:

"Look at that puppy wagging its tail. How do you think it's feeling?" "See those kids on the playground? What do their faces tell us?" "That car just honked its horn. I wonder if that driver is feeling frustrated?"

Make it interactive by sharing your own observations: "When I see those bright flowers, they make me feel happy. What about you?" Let your child lead sometimes too—they might notice things you missed, like a bird singing or someone helping their neighbor carry groceries.

If you spot someone having a tough moment, like a child crying over dropped ice cream, use it as a gentle teaching moment: "That looks hard. Remember when that happened to you? What helped you feel better?"

Keep it light and natural. This isn't a test, just a way to help your child notice and name feelings in everyday life. These little moments of emotional awareness add up, helping your child better understand both their own feelings and those of others.

You can do this anywhere, for example, at the grocery store, in the park, or even looking at family photos at home. The key is making it feel like a game rather than a lesson.

The Emotion Detective Academy: A Parent-Child Investigation Activity

Transform your child into an "Emotion Detective" who investigates feelings through play, storytelling, and creative expression. This activity builds on the concepts of emotional awareness while making the learning process engaging and interactive.

Set-Up

Age range: 4–7 years

Time: 30 minutes initial setup, then 10–15 minutes per daily investigation

Materials needed:

- detective notebook (small notebook or stapled papers)
- magnifying glass (real or paper craft)
- detective badge (crafted from cardboard)
- colored markers/crayons
- magazine pictures of people showing different emotions
- camera or phone for taking photos (optional)
- empty picture frames cut from cardboard

THE INVESTIGATION STATION

Part 1: Detective Training (30 Minutes)

Create your detective kit together:

Design and decorate the detective badge.

Set up the "Investigation Notebook" with sections for:

- "clues" (observed emotional expressions)
- "evidence" (drawings or photos of feelings)
- "case Files" (stories about emotions)

Make a cardboard magnifying glass for "examining" feelings.

Create a "Detective's Oath": "I promise to look for feelings everywhere, To be kind when I find them, And to help others understand them better."

Part 2: Daily Investigations (10–15 Minutes)

Morning Briefing

Start each day by:

- checking your own feelings in the mirror with your magnifying glass.
- recording the "emotional weather" in your notebook.
- setting a daily mission (e.g., "Find three happy moments today").

FIELD ASSIGNMENTS

The story scene investigation

- Look at a picture book together.
- Use the magnifying glass to "search for clues" about characters' feelings.
- Record evidence: Draw the character's face and write/dictate why they might feel that way.

The mirror mystery

- Make different faces in the mirror.
- Take turns guessing each other's emotions.
- Photograph or draw the expressions for your case files.
- Write simple stories about what might have caused these feelings.

The Family feeling forum

- Interview family members about their feelings.
- Record their responses in your notebook.
- Draw pictures of what you discovered.
- Create a "Family Feelings Map".

The emotion collection

- Use your cardboard frames as "emotion catchers".
- Walk around holding up your frame.
- "Capture" different emotional moments you see.
- Draw or describe what you found in your notebook.

Part 3: Detective report time (5 minutes)

End each investigation session by:

- reviewing the day's emotional discoveries.
- adding new findings to your notebook.
- planning tomorrow's mission.
- sharing your favorite discovery of the day.

EXTENSION ACTIVITIES

The Emotion Museum

- Create a gallery of emotional "evidence" collected during investigations.
- Label each piece with the emotion it represents.
- Invite family members to tour the museum.
- Have your child be the museum guide, explaining each exhibit.

Detective Story Time

- Create simple stories about solving "emotion mysteries".
- Example: "The Case of the Grumpy Grandpa" (discovering why Grandpa seems upset).
- Draw pictures to illustrate your cases.
- Share solutions for helping others feel better.

Weekly Case Reviews

- Look through the week's investigations.
- Identify patterns in the emotions discovered.
- Award special "Detective Stars" for:
  - best solution finder
  - most creative investigation
  - kindest response

TIPS FOR PARENTS

- Keep the tone playful and adventurous.
- Validate all emotional discoveries.
- Help connect observations to personal experiences.
- Use detective language to make it fun: "What clues do you see?" "Let's gather more evidence!"
- Celebrate both positive and challenging emotion discoveries.
- Use the magnifying glass as a tool to "zoom in" on subtle expressions.
- Help your child develop their own investigation style.

LEARNING OUTCOMES

Children will develop:

- increased emotional vocabulary.
- better observation of facial expressions and body language.
- greater empathy through perspective-taking.
- confidence in discussing emotions.
- creative problem-solving skills for emotional situations.

Remember to adapt the activity based on your child's interests and attention span. Some children might prefer rapid-fire investigations, while others enjoy longer, more detailed explorations. The key is maintaining engagement while building emotional awareness skills.

Key Takeaways

- ❑ Visual tools like emotion cards and feelings thermometers help children identify and express their emotions more concretely, serving as a bridge for developing emotional language skills.
- ❑ Regular emotional check-ins during natural transitions (like bedtime or breakfast) create opportunities for children to practice recognizing and discussing their feelings in a safe environment.
- ❑ Interactive activities such as "Emotion Detective" games and "Feelings Time Capsules" make emotional learning engaging while helping children develop awareness of both their own emotions and those of others.
- ❑ The goal isn't to eliminate difficult emotions, but to equip children with tools to recognize and manage them effectively, transforming challenging moments into opportunities for connection and growth.

Chapter Three

TEACHING EMOTIONAL REGULATION

Let me tell you about a moment with my nephew Sam that really opened my eyes about kids and emotions. He was having one of those epic meltdowns in the grocery store—you know the kind, where you can feel every parent in the vicinity giving you that sympathetic wince.

Instead of my usual "calm down" I remembered something I'd learned about helping kids handle big feelings. I got down to his level and said, "Looks like your body's feeling really jumpy right now, like there's lightning inside. Want to be storm clouds together?"

His sobs turned to sniffles as we did some "thunder breathing" big deep breaths that we released with quiet rumbles. Before I knew it, we were comparing our bellies to clouds getting bigger and smaller, and he was actually giggling.

It's amazing how kids can learn to handle their emotions when we give them the right tools. Sometimes they just need a different way to think about their feelings, like turning a tantrum into a passing storm.

Calming Techniques: Breathing Exercises, Sensory Tools

Let's explore simple yet effective ways children can manage big emotions through breathing and sensory activities.

Dragon breathing exercise: Transform deep breathing into an adventure–children pretend they're dragons who:

- breathe in deeply through their nose (gathering their dragon power).
- exhale slowly through their mouth (melting imaginary ice castles).
- watch their "dragon breath" disappear in the air.

Nature connection: Getting outside offers natural emotional reset opportunities:

- gentle gardening activities like watering plants
- feeling different textures (smooth leaves, rough bark)
- walking barefoot in grass or sand
- cloud watching for shapes and stories

Safe place visualization: Guide children to create their own mental "calm spot":

- Help them picture their favorite peaceful place (beach, tree house, grandma's garden).
- Add sensory details (what they see, hear, smell, feel).
- Practice visiting this place during quiet moments.

Making It routine: The key is practicing these techniques during calm times:

- Do dragon breaths while waiting for the bus.
- Play texture scavenger hunt during walks.
- Visit their "happy place" as part of bedtime routine.

When children practice these skills regularly, they become natural go-to tools during challenging moments. Keep it playful and consistent, and watch as these techniques become part of their emotional toolkit.

Modeling Emotional Intelligence for Your Children

Share Your Daily Feelings Naturally

During regular moments like dinner or car rides, open up about your emotions: "My meeting was challenging today, but I took deep breaths and found solutions. Sometimes I feel nervous before big presentations, just like you might before a school performance." Keep it simple and authentic. Your child learns most from seeing how you handle real situations.

Navigate Changes Together

When plans fall apart, demonstrate flexible thinking: "The playground is closed? I'm disappointed too. Let's problem-solve together and find another fun activity." Show them that while we can't control everything, we can control our response.

Own Your Mistakes With Grace

Let your children see you acknowledge mistakes and grow from them: "I snapped earlier because I was frustrated. I'm sorry, but I'm learning to take a pause when I feel overwhelmed." This teaches them that mistakes are normal and fixable.

Make Self-Care Visible

Show how you manage your emotions in real-time. Take visible deep breaths, name your feelings out loud, or share simple coping strategies: "I need a quiet moment to reset would you like to practice our calm breathing together?" This demonstrates that everyone needs tools to handle big feelings.

Build Emotional Vocabulary Together

Help children understand the rich world of emotions by naming your own feelings with precision: "I'm not just happy, I'm proud and excited!" or "Right now, I'm feeling both nervous and hopeful about this new project." This helps them develop a nuanced understanding of their own emotional experiences.

THE WEATHER IN MY HEART: A SIMPLE DAILY CHECK-IN

Opening script (2-3 minutes)

"Let's check the weather in our hearts today. First, let's do our thunder breathing together."

- Breathe in like gathering a big storm cloud (4 counts).
- Hold your thunder (2 counts).
- Release it with a gentle rumble (6 counts) (Repeat three times).

Today's weather report (5 minutes)

"Now, tell me about your heart's weather today..."

Encourage descriptions like:

- "sunny skies when playing with friends"
- "a little stormy when sharing was hard"
- "cloudy when missing grandma"

Exploring one weather moment (5 minutes)

Choose one weather event to discuss:

- What brought this weather?
- How did it feel in your body?
- What made it better (for storms) or last longer (for sunshine)?

Tomorrow's weather (2 minutes)

End with hope: "What weather do you hope to create tomorrow?"

TIPS FOR PARENTS

- Keep it playful and natural.
- Use simple weather words for younger children (rain, sun, clouds).
- Add more detailed weather descriptions for older kids (misty, thundery, partly cloudy).
- There's no "bad" weather—all feelings are welcome.

The power of this activity lies in its simplicity. By connecting emotions to familiar weather patterns, children find it easier to express and understand their feelings. Use it daily during a quiet moment, like bedtime or after school, to build emotional awareness together.

Big Kid Feelings Tools (Ages 6-11)

When you're angry or mad

What to try: Count backwards from 20, squeeze a stress ball, or run in place.

Best times to use: During arguments, when losing a game, or when things feel unfair.

When you're worried or nervous

What to try: Box breathing (4-4-4-4), doodle your worries, or name your worry and talk to it.

Best times to use: Before tests, meeting new people, or trying something new.

When you're overwhelmed

What to try: Find five blue things, then four red things, then three yellow things.

Best times to use: too much homework, lots happening at once, can't think clearly.

When you're sad

What to try: Write in your journal, listen to happy music, or talk to a trusted friend.

Best times to use: After disappointments, missing someone, feeling left out.

When you're too energetic

What to try: Shadow boxing with air, silent desk drumming, or stretching exercises.

Best times to use: During quiet time, need to sit still, too much energy inside.

When you're stuck or can't focus

What to try: Take a water break, do 10 jumping jacks, or change your spot.

Best times to use: During homework, when reading, mind feels foggy.

When you have mixed-up feelings

What to try: Draw in different colors, make a feelings playlist, or write a feelings story.

Best times to use: Confusing situations, can't explain feelings, lots of emotions at once.

When you're embarrassed

What to try: Tap your "reset button," say "I can handle this," or take three deep breaths.

Best times to use: After mistakes, awkward moments, when feeling shy.

My Weather Station: An Emotional Awareness Activity Kit

Transform emotion management into an engaging weather-themed experience where children become meteorologists of their feelings. This activity builds on the weather metaphors and breathing techniques from the text while adding interactive elements that make emotional learning concrete and playful.

Set-Up

- Age range: 6–11 years
- Time: 20–30 minutes for initial setup, 5–10 minutes for daily practice
- Materials needed:
    - large poster board for the "Weather Station"
    - blue, white, gray, and yellow construction paper
    - markers or crayons
    - cotton balls for clouds
    - clear plastic pocket or envelope
    - craft supplies (glue, scissors, string)
    - small notebook for "Weather Journal"

THE WEATHER STATION ACTIVITIES

Part 1: Building Your Weather Station (30 minutes)

Create a personal weather monitoring station:

1. **The daily forecast board**

   - Create a large background scene with sky and ground.
   - Make moveable weather elements:
     - cotton ball clouds (happy, calm feelings)
     - gray storm clouds (angry, frustrated feelings)
     - lightning bolts (sudden big feelings)
     - sunshine rays (joyful moments)
     - raindrops (sad feelings)
     - rainbows (mixed feelings)
   - Add a pocket labeled "Today's Weather Pieces".

2. **Weather tools station** Create stations for different emotional weather patterns:

   - thunder breathing cards (illustrated deep breathing steps)
   - stress ball "rain cloud"
   - "lightning rod" (craft stick) for redirecting angry energy
   - happy memory cards
   - gratitude journal
   - "sunshine shortcuts" (quick mood lifters)
   - mixed feelings color wheel
   - emotion word cards
   - "weather report" sentence starters

Part 2: Daily Weather Monitoring

Morning forecast (5 minutes)

1. Check in with your body:

   - Do thunder breathing (big storm cloud breath in, gentle rumble out).
   - Notice where you feel weather in your body.
   - Select weather pieces that match your feelings.
   - Place them on your forecast board.

2. Make your weather prediction:

    - What kind of day do you expect?
    - What weather tools might you need?
    - Write or draw in your Weather Journal.

WEATHER WATCH ACTIVITIES (5-10 MINUTES)

Choose one activity based on current emotional weather:

For stormy weather

- Practice "Storm Breathing":
    a. Gather storm clouds (breathe in).
    b. Hold your thunder (pause).
    c. Release gentle rain (breathe out).
- Use the "Lightning Counter" (counting backward from 20).
- Draw your storm and watch it pass.

For sunny weather

- Share your sunshine (write a kind note).
- Draw sun rays of gratitude.
- Create a "sunny moment" for someone else.

For mixed weather

- Create a rainbow of feelings.
- Use different colors to draw your weather mix.
- Write a weather story about your different feelings.

For cloudy weather

- Practice cloud floating (gentle movement).
- Find shapes in your thought clouds.
- Make a plan to clear some clouds.

Part 3: Evening Weather Report (5 minutes)

1. Review your day's weather:

    o What weather patterns did you notice?
    o Which tools helped the most?
    o What's tomorrow's forecast?

2. Complete your Weather Journal:

    o Draw today's weather journey.
    o Note what helped during weather changes.
    o Plan for tomorrow's weather.

EXTENSION ACTIVITIES

Weekly Weather Maps

- Create a week-long weather tracking chart.
- Look for patterns in your emotional weather.
- Plan ahead for challenging weather.

Weather Reporter Role-Play

- Practice describing feelings as weather.
- Create weather reports for different scenarios.
- Share forecasts with family members.

Weather Tool Testing

- Try different calming techniques.
- Rate how well each tool works.
- Create new tools for your weather station.

TIPS FOR PARENTS

- Keep the atmosphere playful and accepting.
- Validate all types of weather as normal and temporary.
- Help identify early warning signs of brewing storms.
- Practice weather tools during calm moments.

- Share your own weather patterns.
- Celebrate successful weather navigation.

LEARNING OUTCOMES

Children will develop:

- emotional awareness through weather metaphors.
- concrete tools for emotion management.
- vocabulary for expressing feelings.
- understanding of emotional patterns.
- confidence in handling weather changes.

CUSTOMIZATION NOTES

- For younger children: Simplify weather types and focus on basic patterns.
- For older children: Add more complex weather systems and detailed journaling.
- For groups: Create a classroom weather station with individual tracking zones.
- For home use: Incorporate into daily routines like breakfast or bedtime.

Like real weather, emotional weather is ever-changing. The goal isn't to have sunny skies all the time, but to build confidence in handling all types of emotional weather patterns.

Key Takeaways

- ❑ Using weather metaphors (like comparing emotions to storms, sunshine, or clouds) helps children visualize and express their feelings in concrete, understandable ways.
- ❑ Regular practice of calming techniques such as "dragon breathing" or "thunder breathing" during peaceful moments builds emotional regulation skills that children can access during challenging situations.
- ❑ Interactive tools like emotion weather stations, daily check-ins, and sensory activities make emotional learning engaging and help children develop awareness of how feelings manifest in their bodies.

Chapter Four

DEVELOPING EMPATHY AND COMPASSION

Sally noticed her six-year-old son Jake standing quietly by the playground, watching another boy who sat alone on a bench, head down. Before she could say anything, Jake walked over and sat beside him.

"I feel sad sometimes too," she heard Jake say. "Want to build a sandcastle together?"

Later, as they walked home, Sally asked Jake what made him go over there. He shrugged, playing with his jacket zipper. "Remember when I was new at school? Tommy shared his trucks with me. It made me feel better. That boy looked like he needed a friend, too."

Sarah smiled, remembering the countless dinner table conversations where they'd talked about feelings, the pretend play scenarios they'd acted out, and the times she'd pointed out how characters in books might be feeling. In that simple playground moment, she saw all those small lessons coming together.

Growing Kind Hearts: A Family Guide to Building Empathy

Daily "Feelings Finder" Moments

Instead of asking "How do you think they feel?" over and over, make it natural and fun:

During breakfast: "I noticed the crossing guard dancing this morning. She looked so happy! What made you smile today?"

In the car: "That driver let us merge. That was thoughtful! Should we wave thank you?"

While watching TV: "Wow, that character just stood up for their friend. Have you ever done that? How did it feel?"

The Weekly Kind Hearts Challenge

Every Sunday after breakfast, gather around and each person picks one task from these categories:

Helping at home:

- Be someone's "secret helper": Make their bed, organize their desk, or pack their lunch without them knowing.
- Teach something you're good at: Show a younger sibling how to tie shoes or help them with math.
- Give someone a break: Take over a chore that's usually theirs (bonus: leave them a nice note!).
- Create "happy mail": Draw a picture or write a note for someone in the family.

Friendship focus:

- Notice the quiet ones: Say hi to someone who usually plays alone.
- Share the fun: Bring an extra snack for someone who might need it.
- Be a helper: Offer to carry books or explain a tricky homework problem.
- Show you care: Make a card for someone who's having a rough time.

Community kindness:

- Be a neighborhood helper: Pick up litter, bring in trash bins, or water a neighbor's plants.
- Spread joy: Leave positive chalk messages on the sidewalk or happy notes in library books.
- Help the helpers: Make thank-you cards for crossing guards, lunch staff, or janitors.
- Care for creatures: Fill bird feeders or make simple toys for shelter pets.

Monthly Family Project

Pick something that feels meaningful to your family:

- Have a "toy librarian" day: Clean and organize toys to donate.
- Create comfort kits: Pack socks, snacks, and notes for a local shelter.
- Be nature's friends: Clean up a park or plant flowers for bees.
- Welcome wagon: Make welcome packages for new families in the neighborhood.

When Things Get Tough

When siblings argue or feelings get hurt, try this:

- Everyone takes three deep breaths.
- Each person shares their side (set a timer for 1 minute each).
- Brainstorm fixes together: "What would make this better for everyone?"

Tracking Kindness

Keep it simple and visible:

- Hang a basic chart on the fridge.
- Add stickers or checkmarks for completed kind acts.
- Take quick photos of kind moments for a family album.
- Share stories at dinner: "Who did you help today? Who helped you?"

Remember

- Small acts matter, and a smile or "thank you" can change someone's day.
- It's okay to mess up, since we're all learning.
- Notice the ripple effect, for example, how somebody reacts when you're kind to them.
- Celebrate trying to succeed and not only when you achieve something.

The magic happens in tiny moments like when your child shares their cookie without being asked, or comforts a friend who's crying. These small acts build the muscles of empathy that will serve them (and others) throughout their lives.

Quick Win Ideas for Busy Days

- Text a family member just to say "I love you".
- Let someone go ahead of you in line.
- Give a genuine compliment.
- Pick up something someone dropped.
- Share your snack.
- Ask "How are you?" and really listen to the answer.

When kindness becomes part of your daily routine, it becomes part of who your children are.

Kindness Quest: A Family Adventure in Growing Caring Hearts

Transform everyday moments into opportunities for kindness through an engaging quest system that makes empathy and caring feel like an exciting adventure. Based on the story of Jake and the lonely boy at the playground, this activity helps families develop a natural habit of noticing and acting on opportunities for kindness.

Set-Up

- age range: 5-10 years
- time: initial setup 30 minutes, daily quests 5-15 minutes
- materials needed:
    - craft supplies (paper, markers, stickers)
    - small notebook or journal
    - empty jar or box
    - camera (optional)
    - craft materials for badges

The Quest System

Part 1: Creating Your Kindness Command Center (30 minutes)

1. **The quest board.**

    - Create a family display board with sections:

        - active quests (current kindness missions)
        - quest complete! (finished kind acts)
        - kindness heroes (family photos doing kind acts)
        - quest ideas (pocket for new suggestions)

2. **Kindness badges:** Create badges for different types of kind acts:

    - friend maker (like Jake helping the lonely boy)
    - secret helper (anonymous kind acts)
    - joy spreader (making others smile)
    - helper hero (assisting with tasks)
    - nature friend (being kind to environment)
    - family champion (helping at home)

3. **Quest journal:** Each family member gets a small notebook to:

    - record daily kind acts.
    - draw pictures of kind moments.
    - write about how helping others felt.
    - collect "thank you" notes received.

Part 2: Daily Questing (10–15 minutes)

Morning Quest Selection

1. Each family member draws a daily quest card:

    - Spot someone alone (like Jake did).
    - Share something special.
    - Help without being asked.
    - Give a real compliment.
    - Make someone smile.
    - Notice someone's feelings.

2. Quest planning:

   - Discuss how to complete the quest.
   - Share ideas and suggestions.
   - Make any needed preparations.

Evening Quest Review

- Share quest stories at dinner.
- Add completed quests to the board.
- Award appropriate badges.
- Plan next day's adventures.

Part 3: Weekly Special Missions

Choose one bigger mission per week:

School kindness

- Notice who sits alone at lunch.
- Include new students in games.
- Help someone with schoolwork.
- Share school supplies.

Home happiness

- Do secret chores for family.
- Leave happy notes in lunch boxes.
- Help with difficult tasks.
- Create family "thank you" cards.

Neighborhood nice

- Clean up local areas.
- Help elderly neighbors.
- Leave positive chalk messages.
- Share garden flowers.

Community care

- Make cards for essential workers.
- Donate toys or books.
- Help at local events.
- Support local causes.

Extension Activities

Kindness Detective Agency

- Look for "clues" of needed kindness.
- Document kind acts spotted in others.
- Investigate ways to help.
- Report findings at family dinner.

Kindness Story Collection

- Take photos of kind moments.
- Write simple stories about kind acts.
- Create a family kindness book.
- Share stories with relatives.

Kindness Challenge Chain

- Each kind act inspires another.
- Track how kindness spreads.
- See how many people are affected.
- Create a paper chain showing connections.

TIPS FOR PARENTS

- Model noticing opportunities for kindness.
- Share your own kindness stories.
- Make it playful, not pressured.
- Celebrate all attempts at kindness.
- Point out the ripple effects of kind acts.
- Help children process others' reactions.
- Keep a camera ready for kind moments.
- Use dinner time for sharing stories.

LEARNING OUTCOMES

Children will develop

- natural empathy responses
- awareness of others' feelings
- problem-solving for helping others
- confidence in approaching peers
- understanding of community connection
- pride in making a difference

Customization Ideas

For younger children (5-7)

- Simplify quests to basic helping acts.
- Use more pictures, fewer words.
- Focus on immediate family and friends.
- Keep missions very concrete.

For older children (8-10)

- Add more complex community projects.
- Include planning and organization.
- Encourage independent initiatives.
- Add writing and reflection components.

For groups/classrooms

- Create team quests.
- Add cooperative elements.
- Track class-wide impact.
- Develop peer recognition system.

Like Jake's simple act of sitting with a lonely child, the most powerful moments often come from natural, heartfelt responses to others' needs. The quest system simply helps children notice and act on these opportunities more often.

Digital Kindness: Extending Empathy to Online Spaces

As children grow up in an increasingly digital world, teaching empathy must extend beyond face-to-face interactions to online spaces.

Online Empathy Challenges

Children may struggle with digital empathy because:

- They can't see facial expressions or body language.
- There's a sense of distance from the real people behind screens.
- Online culture can sometimes normalize unkindness.
- The immediate reward systems of games and social media can overshadow empathetic choices.

Digital Kindness Activities

Virtual Check-In Circles

Once a week, have a family discussion about online interactions:

- Share a positive online interaction you had or witnessed.
- Discuss a challenging situation and how it could be handled with kindness.
- Role-play responding to difficult messages with empathy.

Screen-to-Heart Connections

Help children understand the real people behind digital interactions:

- When messaging friends or family, discuss how they might feel receiving certain messages.
- Before posting comments, ask yourself how you would feel if someone said this to you.
- Practice pausing before responding when upset online.

Digital Citizenship Projects

- Create family guidelines for kind online behavior.
- Design positive memes or encouraging graphics to share.
- Start a family challenge to send one supportive message daily to friends or family.

Empathy in Gaming

For families with children who enjoy video games:

- Choose cooperative rather than only competitive games.
- Discuss how to be a supportive teammate.
- Talk about how characters in games might feel.
- Practice being a good sport whether winning or losing.

Handling Digital Conflicts With Empathy

When online conflicts arise, guide children through these steps:

- Pause and breathe before responding.
- Consider the other perspective—what might be happening in their life?
- Ask clarifying questions rather than making assumptions.
- Use "I" statements to express feelings without blaming.
- Offer solutions that consider everyone's needs.

Modeling Digital Kindness as Parents

Children learn by watching how adults navigate online spaces:

- Share examples of when you chose kindness online.
- Let children see you supporting others through messages.
- Discuss your own challenges with digital communication.
- Be transparent about mistakes and how you made amends.

Digital Kindness Quest Ideas

Add these to your family's Kindness Quest system:

- Reach out to someone who might feel isolated with a thoughtful message.
- Stand up for someone facing unkindness online (report bullying, send supportive messages).
- Thank the creators of games, videos, or content you enjoy.
- Help someone learn a new digital skill.
- Create and share content that makes others smile.

Tech-Free Balance

Remember that developing empathy also requires face-to-face connection:

- Establish tech-free times for family bonding.
- Practice reading facial expressions and body language.
- Discuss the differences between online and in-person communication.
- Create a balanced "empathy diet" that includes both digital and physical world kindness.

By extending your family's empathy practice to digital spaces, you're preparing children to be compassionate citizens in all the worlds they inhabit—both online and off.

Key Takeaways

- ❏ Digital empathy requires specific attention as children navigate online spaces where facial expressions and body language are absent; activities like "Virtual Check-In Circles" help bridge this gap.
- ❏ Modeling kind behavior, discussing real-life examples, and celebrating small acts of kindness help children internalize empathy as part of their identity rather than viewing it as just another rule to follow.

Chapter Five

SOCIAL SKILLS FOR EMOTIONAL INTELLIGENCE

Helping children learn how to interact well with others is one of the most important things we can teach them. A child who knows how to share, listen, and handle disagreements will likely make friends more easily and feel more confident in social situations. They'll be better equipped to understand not just their own feelings, but also how others might be feeling.

It's also important to teach children about personal space and boundaries. This could be as simple as showing them it's okay to say "no" when they don't want a hug, or helping them recognize when someone else might need space. These lessons help them understand and respect both their own comfort zones and those of others.

We're giving children the tools they need to navigate friendships, handle conflicts, and build positive relationships. Through everyday practice and gentle guidance, they'll gradually develop the social skills that will serve them well throughout their lives.

Conflict Resolution Scripts for Children

You can teach kids to handle conflict through pretend play. For example, you might act out a situation where two friends both want to play with the same toy. Through this kind of practice, kids can try out different ways to solve the problem, for example, like taking turns or finding a way to play together.

After any disagreement (real or pretend), it helps to talk about what happened. Simple questions like "How did you feel?" or "What do you think worked well?" can help kids understand the situation better.

The goal isn't to avoid conflicts altogether they're a normal part of life. Instead, we're helping kids learn to handle disagreements in a way that works for everyone. With practice and patience, they'll develop skills that will help them build stronger friendships and better relationships throughout their lives.

Building Healthy Boundaries and Respecting Others

Every child has their own invisible comfort bubble this is a unique space that defines their personal boundaries. Just as adults have different preferences for personal space and interaction, children naturally vary in how they prefer to connect with others. Understanding and respecting these differences is crucial for healthy social development.

The Foundation of Healthy Boundaries

Children begin learning about boundaries through everyday interactions. When a toddler turns away from a hug or a preschooler declares "mine!" they're actually practicing early boundary-setting. As parents, we can help shape these natural instincts into respectful social skills.

Think about how children interact on a playground—some immediately join group games, while others prefer to watch first. These natural tendencies reveal important information about their comfort zones. Rather than pushing a cautious child to "join in" or telling an enthusiastic hugger to "hold back," we can help them understand and navigate these differences respectfully.

Starting Meaningful Conversations

Opening discussions about boundaries doesn't have to be formal or complicated. Simple questions woven into daily life can spark important insights:

- "How do you feel when someone borrows your toys without asking?"
- "What makes you comfortable or uncomfortable during playtime?"
- "How do you like to say hello to your friends?"

These conversations help children recognize their own preferences while understanding that others might feel differently. When a child realizes their best friend prefers high-fives to hugs, they're learning valuable lessons about respecting individual differences.

The Language of Body Language

One of the most valuable skills we can teach children is how to read and respect non-verbal cues. Help them notice when a friend steps back (needing space), crosses their arms (feeling uncomfortable), or turns away (wanting alone time). Understanding these silent signals helps children navigate social situations more successfully.

Practice identifying these cues in everyday situations:

- When watching TV shows together, point out characters' body language.
- During playdates, help them notice friends' physical signals.
- Share observations about your own body language: "I'm stepping back because I need some space right now".

Building Communication Skills

Equip children with clear, respectful phrases they can use to express their needs and respect others':

- "Can I join your game?"
- "I need some quiet time right now"
- "Would you like a hug or a high-five?"
- "May I borrow that when you're finished?"

These simple phrases give children tools to navigate social situations confidently while respecting others' boundaries.

Learning From Conflicts

Disagreements and boundary crossings are inevitable parts of growing up. Instead of seeing these moments as failures, treat them as valuable learning opportunities. After a conflict has cooled down, guide reflection with thoughtful questions:

- "What were you feeling when it happened?"
- "How do you think your friend was feeling?"
- "What could we try differently next time?"

Encourage creative processing through drawing, storytelling, or role-play. These activities help children understand situations from different perspectives and develop better strategies for next time.

Parents as Role Models

Children learn most powerfully through observation. When they see us respecting boundaries—asking before joining activities, accepting "no" gracefully, expressing our own needs clearly—they internalize these behaviors. Show them how to:

- ask permission before entering personal space
- accept declined invitations with grace
- express needs and preferences clearly
- respect others' "not right now" responses

Creating Lasting Understanding

The goal isn't to create rigid rules about interaction but to help children develop authentic, respectful relationships. When children understand that good friendships include both connection and healthy boundaries, they're better equipped to:

- build meaningful relationships
- stand up for their own needs
- respect others' differences
- navigate social situations confidently

Remember that this learning happens gradually, through daily interactions and gentle guidance. Celebrate small successes, for example, when your child asks before hugging a friend, respects a sibling's need for space, or expresses their own boundaries clearly. These moments show growing emotional intelligence and social awareness.

By helping children understand and respect boundaries, we're giving them essential tools for building healthy relationships throughout their lives. This understanding helps create confident, empathetic individuals who can maintain their own boundaries while respecting those of others.

ACTIVITY: THE FEELINGS AND BOUNDARIES BOARD GAME

This is a fun way to practice social skills.

What you'll need:

- large paper or cardboard for the game board
- markers or crayons
- one die
- game pieces (buttons, toys, or whatever you have)
- cards (can be cut from paper)

Creating your game

- Draw a simple path on your board.
- Color spaces in four different colors.
- Create simple situation cards kids can understand.

Game rules: Roll the dice and move your piece. When you land on a color:

- Red: pick a card and show what you'd do.
- Blue: share a feeling.
- Yellow: show how to ask for space nicely.
- Green: practice joining others' play.

Sample situations for cards:

- "Someone wants to give you a hug."
- "You want to play with a toy someone else has."
- "You see a friend looking sad."
- "Someone joins your game without asking."

Practice phrases: Write these on a helper card for kids to use:

- "Can I play too?"
- "I need some space"
- "Would you like a hug or high-five?"

Playing together:

- Take turns rolling and moving.
- Help each other act out situations.
- Keep it light and fun.
- Praise good ideas and kind responses.

The game can be as simple or creative as you like, and you can add new situations as your child grows.

Tips

- Start with shorter game sessions for younger kids.
- Add more challenging situations for older children.
- Use stuffed animals to act out scenarios.
- Make it silly and fun. Laughter encourages learning.

Key Takeaways

❏ Teaching children to recognize both their own boundaries and others' comfort zones helps them develop healthier relationships and greater social confidence.

❏ Role-playing and practicing conflict resolution through games like "The Feelings and Boundaries Board Game" gives children safe opportunities to develop essential social skills.

❏ Children learn to interpret non-verbal cues and body language through guided observations in everyday situations, TV shows, and playdates.

❏ Parents serve as powerful role models for boundary-setting when they demonstrate respectful behaviors like asking permission, accepting declined invitations gracefully, and clearly expressing their own needs.

Conclusion

Think back to your child's last emotional moment—that broken toy, lost game, or "wrong" color cup. Remember how overwhelming it felt? Now you have tools, strategies, and the understanding to transform these challenging moments into opportunities for growth and connection.

Throughout this book, we've explored how emotional intelligence shapes everything from playground friendships to future relationships. We've learned that it's not about perfect parenting or never having meltdowns, we simply want to work at building understanding.

Your Emotional Intelligence Toolkit

You now have practical strategies to

- navigate big feelings together.
- build empathy through daily conversations.
- create safe spaces for emotional expression.
- model healthy emotional responses.
- turn everyday moments into learning opportunities.

Taking Action Today

Start with these simple steps:

- Begin your day with an emotion check-in.
- Practice one calming strategy together.
- Share a feeling during family dinner.
- Notice and name emotions in others.
- Celebrate small moments of emotional growth.

Remember, emotional intelligence grows gradually, like a garden. Some days will be full of growth and insight; others might feel like starting over. It's all part of the journey. Your consistent presence and support matter more than getting everything "right."

Looking Forward

The skills you're building now will serve your child throughout their life:

- The preschooler who learns deep breathing may become the teenager who handles exam stress well.
- Today's practice in expressing feelings could shape tomorrow's ability to navigate relationships.
- Your modeling of empathy helps develop future leaders and friends who understand and care for others.

Most importantly, remember that this journey isn't just about teaching your child—it's about growing together. As you help your child understand their emotions, you might find yourself developing new insights into your own feelings and reactions.

Every time you acknowledge an emotion, every calm-down corner visit, every conversation about feelings are building blocks for your child's emotional wellbeing. They might seem small now, but they're creating patterns that will last a lifetime.

You don't need to transform everything overnight. Start with one small change today. Notice the tiny victories, for example, when your child uses words instead of actions, shows unexpected kindness, or tries a new way to calm down. These are the moments that matter.

Thank you for taking this journey through emotional intelligence parenting. Keep showing up, keep trying, and remember: you're not just raising a child, but nurturing a heart and mind that will carry these lessons into the future.

Your Next Steps

- ❏ Choose one strategy from this book to try today.
- ❏ Share your learning journey with another parent.
- ❏ Return to this book when you need encouragement or new ideas.
- ❏ Trust that your consistent, loving effort makes a difference.

Every parent-child relationship is unique, and you know your child best. Use these tools and insights in ways that work for your family, adapting and adjusting as needed. You've got this and every small step forward counts.

Book Four

Introduction

You know that moment when you're talking to your kids, and suddenly, you hear your parent's voice coming out of your mouth? It happens to all of us. We tend to parent the same way we were parented, following those deeply ingrained patterns we learned growing up. Here's the important part: We don't have to stay stuck in those patterns. We can choose to do things differently.

Many parents find themselves repeating behaviors they promised they'd never continue. Maybe you've caught yourself raising your voice just like your dad did, or using those same phrases your mom always used that drove you crazy. It's a common experience that can leave us feeling frustrated and disappointed in ourselves. Understanding that this is a normal part of parenting is the first step toward making changes.

Being more mindful as a parent doesn't require perfection. Instead, it's about becoming aware of our reactions and taking that crucial pause before responding to our children. It's about recognizing those moments when our own childhood experiences are influencing how we parent today. When we understand where our parenting patterns come from, we can start making different choices that better align with the parent we want to be.

Our own childhood experiences shape us more than we realize. If you grew up with critical parents, you might find yourself being overly critical of your kids without meaning to be. If your emotions were often dismissed as a child, you might struggle to validate your children's feelings now. These patterns run deep, but becoming aware of them is the first step toward healing and change.

Making changes in our parenting style starts with simple, practical steps. When your child does something that triggers you, try to pause and take a breath before reacting. Ask yourself if your response is coming from a thoughtful place, or if it's just an automatic reaction based on how you were parented. Consider what you needed as a child in similar situations, and try to provide that for your own children now.

This journey isn't about criticizing how our parents raised us. Most of them did the best they could with what they knew at the time. Instead, it's about recognizing that we now have the opportunity to do things differently, to create a more understanding and emotionally healthy environment for our children. We can learn from the past without being bound by it.

Good parenting isn't about getting everything right all the time. It's about being present, listening more than lecturing, trying to understand before reacting, and being willing to apologize when we make mistakes. It's about showing our children that it's okay to have feelings and teaching them healthy ways to express them. Most importantly, it's about taking care of our own emotional health so we can be there for our kids in the ways they need us to be.

Changing old patterns isn't easy, and it won't happen overnight. Like breaking in a new pair of shoes, new parenting approaches might feel uncomfortable at first. You'll probably slip back into old habits sometimes, and that's okay. What matters is your commitment to keep trying, to keep walking this new path even when it feels challenging.

As you work on healing your own emotional wounds and changing old patterns, you're teaching your children valuable life lessons. They're learning how to handle difficult emotions, solve problems thoughtfully, and build strong relationships. They're seeing firsthand that it's possible to break free from unhealthy family patterns and create positive change.

Remember, you don't have to figure everything out on your own. Reach out to friends, join parenting groups, or work with a counselor. Sometimes, just knowing that other parents face similar struggles can help you feel less alone and more hopeful about making changes. Share your experiences, learn from others, and gather new ideas to try with your own family.

Every day brings a fresh opportunity to parent differently. Some days will go better than others, and that's perfectly normal. What matters most is your awareness and your commitment to creating positive changes. Your children don't need you to be a perfect parent, but rather to be present, caring, and willing to grow alongside them.

By choosing to parent differently, you're not just changing things for your own children, you're helping to create a better future for generations to come. Every time you respond with patience instead of anger, or understanding instead of criticism, you're helping to write a new family story. It's a story of healing, growth, and breaking free from old patterns to create something better. This is how real, lasting change happens.

Chapter One

RECOGNIZING GENERATIONAL PATTERNS

The words escaped my mouth before I could catch them: "Because I said so!" I froze, coffee mug halfway to my lips, as my eight-year-old daughter stormed off to her room. In that moment, I heard my mother's voice in my own, and behind that, like an echo through time, my grandmother's. Three generations of women, all reaching for the same worn-out phrase when frustration peaked.

Later that evening, as I sat on the edge of my daughter's bed, I remembered how much I'd hated hearing those words as a child. "I'm sorry about earlier," I told her, looking at her sketching in her notebook. "I'd like to hear why you disagree with me about screen time." Her pencil stopped moving, and she looked up, surprised. In that small moment of choosing to listen instead of dismiss, I felt something shift; a tiny break in a pattern that had run through our family for generations. While my grandmother and mother had given me so many wonderful things, some habits needed to be changed.

Understanding Family Patterns and Cultural Influences in Parenting

Our parenting style is shaped by two powerful forces: the patterns we inherited from our own families and the cultural context we live in. Understanding how these forces work together can help us make more conscious choices about how we raise our children.

How Family Patterns and Culture Shape Our Parenting

Think about the last time you responded to your child with a phrase that made you think, "I sound just like my mother!" These moments reveal how deeply our family patterns and cultural background influence our parenting choices. Whether it's how we handle discipline, show affection, or respond to achievements, we often unconsciously follow scripts learned from our own upbringing and cultural environment.

For example, if you grew up in a family that highly valued academic achievement, you might find yourself feeling anxious about your child's grades, even if you consciously want to be more relaxed about schooling. Or if your culture emphasizes respect for elders, you might struggle with allowing your children to express disagreement, even when you want to encourage open communication.

Modern parents face unique challenges in navigating these inherited patterns:

- Social media creates pressure to parent in certain ways, often conflicting with traditional approaches.
- Changing family structures (single parenting, multi-generational homes, blended families) require adapting traditional practices.
- Cultural expectations may clash with contemporary parenting knowledge.
- Different approaches between partners can create tension, especially in intercultural families.

Making Conscious Parenting Choices: A Guided Reflection Exercise

This exercise will help you identify and examine your inherited parenting patterns. Set aside 30 minutes in a quiet space with a journal.

Part 1: Mapping Your Family's Parenting Language (15 minutes)

Answer these specific questions about three generations:

Your grandparents:

- What phrases did they commonly use with your parents?
- How did they show love and affection?
- What were their rules about behavior?
- How did they handle discipline?

Your parents:

- What phrases did they frequently say to you?
- How did they praise or criticize?
- What were their expectations about achievement?
- How did they respond when you were upset?

Your current parenting:

- Which phrases from your parents do you catch yourself repeating?
- What parenting moments make you feel most triggered?
- How do you show love to your children?
- What are your automatic responses to misbehavior?

Part 2: Cultural Influences Assessment (10 minutes)

For each parenting practice below, note whether it comes from your family tradition, cultural background, or modern influences:

1. Discipline approaches.

    - How do you typically respond to misbehavior?
    - Where did you learn this approach?
    - Does it align with your current values?

2. Expression of emotions.

    - How comfortable are you with your children expressing different emotions?
    - How does this compare to your family's approach?
    - What cultural messages influence your response?

3. Achievement and success.

    - What expectations do you have for your children's achievements?
    - How do these align with your cultural background?
    - What would you like to do differently?

Part 3: Creating Your Parenting Path (5 minutes)

Choose three specific parenting situations you frequently encounter. For each one:

1. Write down your typical response.

2. Identify where this response comes from (family pattern or cultural influence).
3. Decide if you want to
   - keep this approach.
   - modify it slightly.
   - create a completely new response.

Create an action plan for each situation you want to change:

- What specific trigger situations do you want to handle differently?
- What new response would you like to try?
- What support do you need to make this change?

Weekly Check-In Questions

Review these questions each week:

- What inherited pattern did I notice myself following this week?
- How did my cultural background influence my parenting choices?
- What one small change did I try?
- How did my children respond to this change?
- What support do I need to continue making conscious parenting choices?

The goal isn't to reject all inherited patterns or cultural influences, but to consciously choose which ones serve your family well. Some traditional practices might carry valuable wisdom, while others may need updating for your family's current context.

Building Support

Consider finding a "parenting reflection partner" or another parent who's also working on examining their parenting patterns. Schedule regular check-ins to:

- share successes in trying new approaches
- discuss challenges in changing old patterns
- explore how cultural expectations affect your parenting
- exchange resources and ideas for conscious parenting

This journey of examining and adjusting your parenting patterns takes time and patience. Start with small changes, celebrate progress, and be compassionate with yourself as you work to create the parenting approach that best fits your family.

Breaking and Building: Creating Your Family Legacy

When Alice first realized she was using her mother's exact tone to address her son's messy room, she felt trapped in a cycle she had promised herself she would break. "It wasn't just the words," she explains, "but the underlying message that order was more important than his creative process." As the daughter of immigrants who had sacrificed everything for stability, Alice understood where this value came from, yet she wanted to honor her son's different needs.

This tension between honoring our roots and creating something new defines the modern parenting journey. We stand at a unique crossroads where we can consciously shape our family legacies.

The Both/and Approach

Tomas and Lucia struggled with different cultural expectations around mealtime. Tomas grew up in a household where children ate whatever was served without complaint, while Lucia's family encouraged expressing preferences and helping with meal planning. Their solution? Creating what they call "both/and" parenting.

"Monday through Thursday, we follow the more traditional approach where everyone eats the same meal," explains Lucia. "But weekends are 'family choice' days where our children take turns helping plan and prepare meals." This approach honors Tomas's cultural values around respect and gratitude while incorporating Lucia's emphasis on voice and choice.

This "both/and" thinking helps parents move beyond the false choice between tradition and innovation. You can maintain your cultural foundations while adapting them to your family's unique needs.

Small Moments, Big Changes

The most profound parenting shifts often happen in ordinary moments. For James, it was catching himself about to dismiss his daughter's fear of swimming, just as his father had dismissed his childhood fears. Instead of saying, "There's nothing to be afraid of," he paused and asked, "What part feels scary to you?"

"That tiny pivot changed everything," James shares. "Instead of pushing through her fear, we talked about it. We made a plan together. She still learned to swim, but she did it feeling supported instead of shamed. That's the legacy I want to leave."

These small course corrections accumulate over time, gradually creating new family patterns that your children may someday pass to theirs.

Permission to Be Imperfect

Perhaps the most important element in conscious parenting is giving yourself permission to be imperfect in the process. Sarla, a mother of three, describes how liberating it felt when she started acknowledging her mistakes to her children.

"I grew up believing parents had to appear infallible," she explains. "But when I started saying 'I made a mistake, let me try again,' my relationship with my kids improved, and they became more willing to acknowledge their own mistakes."

This willingness to be vulnerable and to admit when we slip into old patterns and to try again models the very resilience and growth mindset we hope to instill in our children.

Your Evolving Family Story

Consider your family story as a book that's still being written. The early chapters like your childhood, your cultural background, your family patterns provide important context, but you get to write the next chapters.

Lin, a father who grew up with emotionally distant parents, describes this process: "I'm keeping the chapters about hard work and responsibility that my parents wrote, but I'm adding new ones about emotional connection and playfulness. My children will inherit a more complete story."

As you continue your journey of examining and reshaping your parenting patterns, remember that you're not erasing your history but adding to it—taking the best of what came before while courageously creating something new that reflects your deepest values and responds to your children's unique needs.

Key Takeaways

- ❏ Our parenting approaches are heavily influenced by both family patterns and cultural context, often causing us to unconsciously repeat phrases and behaviors from our own upbringing.
- ❏ Conscious parenting involves recognizing when we're following inherited patterns, reflecting on whether they align with our current values, and deliberately choosing which traditions to keep or modify.
- ❏ The "both/and" approach offers a balanced path forward, maintaining valuable cultural foundations while adapting them to meet our family's unique needs rather than feeling forced to choose between tradition and innovation.
- ❏ Small, intentional changes in everyday moments (like choosing to listen instead of dismiss) can gradually break generational patterns and create a new family legacy that combines the best of our heritage with our own values.

Chapter Two

HEALING YOUR INNER CHILD

I found the box while looking for my winter boots. Emma was in her room, hosting what sounded like the world's most dramatic tea party for her dolls, so I figured I had a few minutes to peek inside.

There it was, at the very bottom: my third-grade school photo. God, those pigtails. I'd been so proud of doing them myself that morning, even though one sat about two inches higher than the other. How the other girls laughed at me during lunch, the hot shame creeping up my neck, Mom's voice later that night: "You've got to learn to be tougher, Susan. The world doesn't have time for sensitive kids."

Just this morning, Emma had bounced into the kitchen wearing striped socks that didn't match and her t-shirt on backward, twirling like she'd just invented clothes. The words had been right there, ready to tumble out "Honey, go fix your shirt." But I'd stopped myself, grabbed my phone instead, and took her photo.

Sitting on my closet floor, holding that old photo, I wondered what my mom would think of Emma's backward shirt. More importantly, I wondered what that gap-toothed little girl with the crooked pigtails would think of how her daughter gets to be exactly who she is.

Building Emotional Resilience: A Practical Guide for Parents

Quick-Start Healing Activities

ACTIVITY 1: GUIDED LETTER WRITING (15 MINUTES)

Start with these sentence prompts to explore your parenting journey:

Dear younger me,

- I want you to know that...
- What happened wasn't your fault because...
- I'm proud of how you...
- The strength you showed when...
- I promise to give my children what you needed most, which was...
- The way you handled... taught me to be a better parent by...

ACTIVITY 2: PATTERN RECOGNITION (10 MINUTES)

Complete these statements to identify recurring patterns:

- When my child gets upset, I usually...
- I learned this response from...
- A different way I could handle this is...
- When I'm stressed, I tend to...
- This reminds me of how my family...
- I'd like to respond instead by...

Understanding Our Parenting Journey

Our past experiences shape how we parent, but we don't need to stay stuck in old patterns. Each day brings new opportunities to choose how we want to respond to our children. The activities above help us recognize these patterns so we can make conscious choices about our parenting approach.

Building Your Support Network: A 5-Day Practice

DAY 1: STARTING SMALL

Today's actions:

- Send a text to one parent friend.
- Join one online parenting group.
- Write down three places you regularly see other parents (school pickup, park, etc.).

Evening check-in:

- What felt easy about connecting today?
- What felt challenging?
- What's one thing you'll try tomorrow?

DAY 2: STRENGTHENING CONNECTIONS

Choose two of these actions:

- Comment on someone's post in your parenting group.
- Strike up a conversation at pickup or the playground.
- Share one parenting challenge you're facing with a trusted friend.
- Offer help to another parent.

DAY 3: CREATING REGULAR CONNECTION POINTS

Pick one to establish:

- weekly: parent-child playdate
- monthly: coffee with another parent
- online: daily check-in with a parenting group

DAY 4: DEEPENING SUPPORT

Today's focus is quality conversations.

- Share something meaningful about your parenting journey.
- Ask another parent about their challenges.
- Offer specific support ("Can I pick up your kid with mine on Thursday?").

DAY 5: MAINTAINING MOMENTUM

Create your ongoing connection plan:

- daily: quick check-in with one parent friend
- weekly: one in-person parent meeting
- monthly: group activity or playdate

Practical Tools for Tough Moments

QUICK GROUNDING EXERCISES

When parenting triggers old wounds:

- Take three deep breaths.
- Name five things you can see.
- Remember: "I'm parenting in the present, not the past".
- Ask yourself: "What does my child need right now?"

SUPPORT SYSTEM CHECKLIST

Build your parenting village with these specific steps:

Immediate support:

- Save three parent friends' numbers in your "favorites".
- Join two local parenting groups (online or in-person).
- Identify one professional resource (counselor, parent coach, etc.).

Weekly connection plan:

- Monday: text check-in with parent friend
- Wednesday: playground meet up
- Friday: online group participation
- Weekend: family activity with another family

Making It Work: Real-Life Strategies

FOR BUSY PARENTS

- Use school pickup time for quick connections.
- Turn errands into meet ups ("Want to grocery-shop together?").
- Create a text group for sharing daily wins and challenges.

FOR INTROVERTS

- Start with online communities.

- Plan one-on-one playdates instead of large groups.
- Set boundaries about connection time ("I can chat for 15 minutes").

FOR WORKING PARENTS

- Schedule virtual coffee dates during lunch breaks.
- Create a weekend parent group.
- Use voice messages for connection during commutes.

Weekly Check-In Questions

Review these every Sunday:

- What support did I receive this week?
- What support did I give?
- Where do I need more help?
- What's one connection I'll prioritize next week?

Remember

- Building support takes time.
- Start with one small connection.
- Quality matters more than quantity.
- It's okay to ask for help.
- Your children benefit from seeing you build connections.

Action Steps for Tomorrow

- Send one supportive message to another parent.
- Schedule one parent meet up for next week.
- Join one local or online parenting group.
- Write down your three most supportive parent friends.
- Plan one self-care activity with support from your village.

The journey of parenting doesn't have to be walked alone. Each small step toward connection builds a stronger foundation for both you and your children.

Breaking Cycles and Building Support

Part 1: Reflecting on Your Parenting Patterns

MEMORY MAPPING

Think about a recent interaction with your child that triggered a strong emotional response in you:

What happened?

_____
_____

How did you feel in that moment?

_____
_____

Did this remind you of any childhood experiences?

_____
_____

How did you respond to your child?

_____
_____

How would you like to have responded?

_____
_____

Connecting past to present. Complete these sentences:

When my child shows strong emotions, I typically feel:

_____
_____

This may connect to how emotions were handled in my childhood by:

_____
_____

One pattern from my upbringing that I want to change is:

_____
_____

One tradition or approach from my family that I want to preserve is:

_____
_____

Part 2: Healing Letter Exercise

Write a brief letter to your younger self about a challenging childhood moment. Include:

- what you wish someone had told you then
- what you've learned since that time
- how you're trying to parent differently now

Dear younger me,

_____
_____

Part 3: Response Planning

Identify your triggers. List three situations that commonly trigger automatic reactions:

_____
_____

Create new responses. For each trigger above, plan an alternative response:

Instead of _____, I will try _____

Instead of _____, I will try _____

Instead of _____, I will try _____

Quick grounding practice. Design your personal 30-second reset for tough parenting moments:

Deep breaths: How many?

_____

_____

A phrase to tell yourself:

_____

_____

Physical action (stretch, touch something, etc.):

_____

_____

Part 4: Building Your Support Network

Current connections assessment. Rate your current support level from 1-10: ____

Who are three people you can reach out to about parenting challenges?

1. _____ Contact: _____

2. _____ Contact: _____

3. _____ Contact: _____

Connection planning. Choose options that feel manageable for you:

☐ daily: quick text check-in with one parent friend
☐ weekly: brief in-person connection (school pickup, playground, etc.)
☐ monthly: scheduled parent meet up or activity
☐ online: joining a supportive parenting community

My first three steps: List three specific actions you'll take in the next week to build your support:

When will you do each one? (Be specific about day/time)

Part 5: Celebrating Small Wins

This week's moments of growth. Note one moment where you:

Responded differently than your parents might have:

_____
_____

Connected meaningfully with another parent:

_____
_____

Showed yourself compassion during a parenting challenge:

_____
_____

Tracking your journey. What differences have you noticed in:

How your child responds to you:

_____
_____

How you feel about parenting challenges:

_____
_____

Your ability to reach out for support:

_____
_____

Part 6: My Parenting Affirmations

Create three simple statements to remind yourself of your parenting values:

WEEKLY CHECK-IN QUESTIONS

Set aside 10 minutes each week to reflect:

- What parenting pattern did I notice myself repeating or changing?
- What support did I receive or give this week?
- Where do I need more help or resources?
- What's one small step I can take next week?

Remember

- Healing happens in small moments, not all at once.
- Connection doesn't have to be perfect to be valuable.
- You're not just raising your children, you're also reparenting yourself.
- Every time you choose a new response, you're breaking cycles.
- You deserve support on this journey.

Key Takeaways

- ❏ Our past experiences and childhood wounds significantly influence our parenting responses, often causing us to automatically react in ways similar to how we were parented.
- ❏ Breaking generational cycles requires conscious awareness of our triggers, planned alternative responses, and regular reflection on the patterns we want to change or preserve.
- ❏ Building a strong support network through consistent connections with other parents (whether through text check-ins, playdates, or online communities) is essential for sustainable parenting growth.
- ❏ Small, intentional daily choices like celebrating a child's unique self-expression instead of correcting it create powerful shifts in both our parenting approach and our own healing journey.

Chapter Three

MINDFUL PARENTING IN ACTION

The morning was its usual chaos. Breakfast dishes in the sink, work emails piling up, and Tommy wrestling with his shoelaces on the bottom step. My hand twitched toward my phone, already running through the day's meetings in my head. I already knew we were going to be late.

Something made me stop. Maybe it was the way his little shoulders were hunched, or how his fingers trembled slightly with each try at the laces. Instead of swooping in to fix it like I usually would, I just... sat down next to him.

"Those things are a pain, huh?"

He glanced up, clearly waiting for me to take over. When I didn't, he went back to concentrating, tongue stuck out slightly at the corner of his mouth. "Watch this, Mom," he whispered, looping one lace over the other. "I've been practicing."

For once, I wasn't half-listening while scrolling through emails or mentally updating my to-do list. I just watched his hands work, noticed how much bigger they seemed than last month.

When he finally pulled those loops tight, the smile that lit up his face caught me off guard. Funny how the biggest moments sometimes come disguised as the smallest ones.

Enhancing Empathy in Parent-Child Interactions

Have you ever wondered why some days it feels like you and your child are speaking different languages? The good news is that building a better connection with your child isn't rocket science.

Let's start with really listening to your child. We're not talking about the "uh-huh" kind of listening while scrolling through your phone. Think about those moments when your child comes home from school bubbling with excitement or clearly upset about something. Try putting your phone away, turning away from the stove for a moment, and giving them your full attention. It's amazing how much more kids share when they feel you're truly listening to them.

Next time your child is telling you about their day, try sitting at their eye level and just letting them talk without jumping in to fix things or give advice. You might be surprised by how much more they open up.

Understanding your child's perspective is another game-changer. When your six-year-old has a meltdown over a broken crayon, your first thought might be "it's just a crayon!" Try to remember what it feels like to be six, when a broken crayon might feel like the end of the world. Taking a moment to understand why something matters to your child can make a huge difference in how you respond.

Clear communication goes both ways. Instead of saying "Stop being difficult!" when your child won't get ready for bed, try "I can see you're having fun playing. Would you like five more minutes before bedtime?" This kind of talking helps keep everyone calmer and shows your child how to express themselves better too.

Finally, take a few minutes at the end of each day to think about your interactions with your child. Maybe while you're doing the dishes or getting ready for bed, ask yourself: "What went well today? What could I have handled differently?"

What works for one child might not work for another even within the same family! The key is to keep trying these approaches, adjust them to fit your family's style, and be patient with the process. Small changes in how we listen, understand, and talk to our kids can make a difference over time.

Mindful Parenting: A Practical Guide for Busy Families

Quick-Start Mindfulness Strategies by Time of Day

Mindful Mornings

- Set a gentle tone with three calm breaths together.
- Create a "quiet corner" for peaceful breakfast time.
- Use visual schedules to reduce rushing.
- Keep phones in another room until breakfast is done.

Quick fix for morning rush:

- Stop and take one deep breath.
- Get at child's eye level.
- State observation: "I see we're running late".
- Offer choices: "Would you like to finish your toast or get dressed first?"
- Set a fun timer: "Let's see if we can be ready before this song ends."

Mindful Mealtimes

- Place phones in a designated basket.
- Share one highlight from your day.
- Practice "one bite, one breath" eating.
- Use conversation starter cards.
- Notice food colors, textures, and flavors together.

Mindful Movement and Play

- Designate 15 minutes for undivided attention play.
- Follow your child's lead in activities.
- Narrate what you observe: "I see you building carefully".
- Practice peaceful pauses between activities.
- Use transition warnings: "Five more minutes of play".

Mindful Bedtime Rituals

- Create a calm-down corner with soft lighting.
- Read together with different character voices.
- Share three gratitudes from the day.
- Practice "starfish breathing" (spread fingers with each breath).
- End with a peaceful phrase: "Peace begins with me".

Mindfulness During Challenging Moments

When Conflicts Arise

- Pause and breathe.
- Name the emotions: "I notice you're feeling frustrated".
- Validate feelings: "It's okay to feel upset".
- Offer calm-down tools: "Should we use our breathing ball?"
- Problem-solve together: "What could we try next time?"

For Overwhelming Moments

- Step away for a 30-second reset.
- Use the "STOP" method:
  - Stop what you're doing.
  - Take a breath.
  - Observe your thoughts and feelings.
  - Proceed mindfully.
- Model self-regulation: "I need a moment to calm my body".

7-Day Mindful Parenting Challenge

Day 1: Morning Mindfulness

- Create a peaceful morning routine.
- Practice: 3-minute morning check-in.
- Evening reflection: how did the morning feel different?

Day 2: Mindful Listening

- Practice full attention during conversations.
- Don't multitask while your child is telling you a story.
- What did you learn by listening deeply?

Day 3: Mindful Meals

- Eat one device-free meal.
- Share favorite moments from the day.
- How did connection feel different?

Day 4: Mindful Play

- Practice 15 minutes of child-led play.
- Notice their play without directing them.
- What did you discover about your child?

Day 5: Mindful Emotions

- Name feelings experienced throughout the day.
- Notice how others are feeling.
- What emotions were most common?

Day 6: Mindful Movement

- Dance, stretch, or walk together.
- Practice noticing body sensations.
- How did movement affect mood?

Day 7: Mindful Gratitude

- Share moments you appreciated.
- "I'm grateful for you because…"
- How has the week changed your connection?

Making Mindfulness Sustainable

Choose Your Daily Non-Negotiables

Pick three mindful moments to practice every day:

- morning connection (three minutes)
- one mindful meal
- bedtime gratitude

Track Your Progress

Use this simple daily check-in:

- today's wins
- tomorrow's intention
- one thing I learned

Family Involvement

- Create a "mindful moments" jar.
- Add notes about special connections.
- Read them together weekly.
- Let children add their own observations.
- Celebrate mindful choices together.

Remember

- Start small with three-minute practices.
- Choose one routine to make mindful.
- Notice improvement, not perfection.
- Return to breathe when overwhelmed.
- Model self-compassion when you forget.

Quick Reference Guide

Mindful Phrases to Use Daily

- "Let's take a breath together."
- "I notice you're feeling…"
- "Would you like to try…"
- "Let's pause for a moment."
- "I'm here with you."

Signs You Need a Mindful Moment

- rising voice
- tense shoulders
- racing thoughts
- rushing movements
- repeating yourself

Simple Reset Tools

- Take three deep breaths.
- Count to ten.
- Touch something soft.
- Look out a window.
- Hum a favorite song.

The journey to mindful parenting is ongoing. Each small moment of presence builds stronger family connections and more peaceful days.

When Technology Meets Mindfulness: Finding Balance in a Digital World

In today's world, completely unplugging isn't realistic for most families. Between work emails, school portals, and the occasional sanity-saving YouTube video when you need to make dinner, technology is part of family life. The goal isn't to eliminate screens entirely but to find a mindful balance that works for your family.

The Reality Check

I realized how much had changed when my daughter asked me to "pause" our conversation so she could finish watching a video. That moment hit me hard. I'd been so focused on limiting screen time that I hadn't taught her how to transition between digital and real-world connections.

Mindful Tech Habits for Families

Create Digital Transition Rituals

Just as we have bedtime routines, create small rituals for moving between screen time and family time:

"When we put our tablets away, let's do three big stretches together."

"After this show ends, we'll make a snack together before starting homework."

"Let's play 'two truths and a wish' after devices go off at dinner."

These simple bridges help everyone's brains adjust from digital stimulation to human connection.

Tech-Free Zones That Actually Work

Instead of fighting a losing battle against screens everywhere, designate certain spaces as naturally screen-free:

The dinner table: Place a pretty basket nearby where everyone (yes, parents too) deposits devices before eating.

Bedrooms at night: Create charging stations in common areas to avoid the "just one more video" temptation.

The car: For short trips, try "car karaoke" or "I spy" instead of defaulting to screens.

The Power of "Tech And" Instead of "Tech Or"

Rather than seeing technology as the opposite of connection, try combining them:

"Let's look up a cookie recipe together, then bake it." "Can we find a nature scavenger hunt app for our walk tomorrow?" "Should we video chat with Grandma while we build this Lego set?"

When You've Had a "Too Much Screen Time" Day

We all have those days when screens took over more than we'd like. Instead of parent guilt, try this reset:

- Take a deep breath and remind yourself that one day doesn't define your parenting.
- Spend 10 minutes in fully present connection before bedtime.
- Say to your child: "I love talking with you even more than any show or game".
- Set one simple intention for tomorrow.

Small Moments Matter Most

Last week, my son and I were both scrolling on our devices in the living room when our eyes met over our screens. Something about the absurdity of sitting three feet apart, but mentally miles away, made us both laugh. I put my phone down and asked, "Want to build a blanket fort instead?"

That spontaneous fort became our new favorite reading spot, and now when either of us says, "fort time," it's our code for "let's connect without screens."

The truth is, mindful parenting isn't about perfection. It's about noticing when we've drifted and gently finding our way back to each other, one small moment at a time.

Remember

- Technology itself isn't good or bad. It's about how mindfully we use it.
- Your children are learning digital habits by watching yours.
- Connection can happen in small, ordinary moments.
- Each day offers new opportunities to reset.

As you continue on your mindful parenting journey, be gentle with yourself. In a world pulling our attention in a thousand directions, simply noticing when you've drifted and choosing to return to presence with your child might be the most powerful gift you can give them and yourself.

Key Takeaways

- ❏ Small moments of full presence, like sitting with a child struggling with shoelaces instead of rushing to help create meaningful connections that are easily missed when parents are distracted by devices or busy schedules.
- ❏ Integrating simple mindfulness practices into daily routines (like morning breathing exercises, device-free meals, and bedtime gratitude rituals) helps families establish sustainable habits rather than seeing mindfulness as another overwhelming task.
- ❏ Creating intentional "digital transition rituals" helps bridge the gap between screen time and real-world connections, making it easier for both parents and children to shift their attention and engage meaningfully with each other.
- ❏ Mindful parenting isn't about perfection but about recognizing when attention has drifted and gently returning to the present. Each reset is an opportunity to model self-compassion and strengthen family bonds.

Chapter Four

TRANSFORMING DISCIPLINE INTO TEACHING

Maya was zooming down the hallway, her science project clutched against her chest, when it happened. The blue ceramic vase that had sat on the shelf forever lay scattered across the floor in pieces. Her stomach dropped as she heard Mrs. Rodriguez's footsteps approaching from the classroom.

Instead of the lecture she was dreading, Mrs. Rodriguez just pulled up two chairs. "Come sit with me for a minute," she said, and weirdly, she didn't even sound mad.

"I was just... I wanted to show you my project," Maya mumbled, staring at her shoes. "The one about plant growth? I got all the seeds to sprout and..."

"That sounds amazing," Mrs. Rodriguez said. "And you know what? I love how excited you are about science. But let's figure out a way to keep you safe while you're sharing your discoveries, okay?"

Maya looked up, surprised. "Maybe... I could walk? Even when I'm super excited?"

"That's a great start. And where do you think would be a good spot for backpacks so they're not near the shelves?"

Developing Positive Reinforcement Techniques

Remember the last time your kid had a total meltdown in the grocery store? Or when they refused to share their toys for the hundredth time? Instead of jumping straight to time-outs or taking away privileges, let's talk about turning these tough moments into chances for growth.

Think about how you feel when your boss only points out your mistakes, versus when they notice your hard work. Kids aren't so different. When we make a big deal about the good stuff, for example, when they help their little sister without being asked, or when they remember to hang up their backpack, they're more likely to repeat it. It's not about bribing them; it's about showing them that good choices lead to good feelings.

You don't need an elaborate system to make this work. Maybe it's a simple chart on the fridge where they earn stars for helping with dishes or being kind to their sibling. Ten stars might mean getting to pick the movie for family night or staying up 15 minutes later. The key is letting them help decide the rewards.

Instead of just saying "good job", try being specific. "I saw how you helped your friend up when she fell at the playground" means more than "you're being nice." It helps kids understand exactly what they did right, making them more likely to repeat it. This kind of specific praise builds their confidence and helps them understand what behaviors we value.

Let's say your kid pushes another child at the park. The old way might be instant punishment: "Go sit on the bench!" The new way? "Let's talk about what happened. Were you feeling frustrated? What else could you do next time?" It's not about letting them off the hook, but about teaching them how to handle tough situations better next time. When we take time to discuss what happened, kids learn to think through their actions and understand their consequences.

In real life, this might look like waiting until your child is calm after a meltdown, then talking about better ways to express big feelings. It might mean creating simple routines with clear rewards, like earning screen time by completing homework without complaints. Try to catch them being good at least three times for every one time you need to correct behavior. Make a habit of asking "what could we do differently next time?" after mistakes.

Building Better Behaviors: A Teaching-First Approach to Discipline

When children test boundaries or make mistakes, we have an opportunity to teach rather than simply punish. Let's explore how to transform challenging moments into learning experiences.

The Teaching Mindset

Instead of seeing misbehavior as something to correct, view it as a skill gap to address. Just as we wouldn't punish a child for not knowing multiplication, we can approach behavioral challenges as teaching opportunities.

From Punishment to Learning: Everyday Examples

THE PLAYGROUND PUSH TRADITIONAL: IMMEDIATE TIME-OUT TEACHING APPROACH:

Wait for everyone to be calm.

"I noticed you pushed when Sam took the swing. What were you feeling?"

"Let's practice ways to say 'I was using that' or find a teacher when you're upset"

Role-play the situation together.

THE HOMEWORK BATTLE TRADITIONAL

Lost privileges teaching approach:

- Break tasks into manageable chunks.
- Create a visual schedule together.
- Celebrate small completions: "You finished math before break. Your planning really worked!"
- Discuss what makes homework challenging and brainstorm solutions together.
- Sibling conflicts traditional approach: separating kids without discussion.

Teaching approach:

- Guide conflict resolution: "Let's hear both sides"
- Help identify feelings: "You seem frustrated because..."
- Practice sharing solutions: "What could work for both of you?"
- Notice and praise cooperative moments.

Building Positive Patterns

Specific praise: Instead of: "Good job!" Try: "You remembered to ask your sister before using her art supplies. That shows real respect for her belongings."

Natural consequences: Instead of: "No TV because you didn't clean up" Try: "We spent so much clean-up time that we ran out of time for TV. Tomorrow, if we work together to tidy up quickly, we'll have time for a show."

Family Problem-Solving

- Hold regular family meetings to discuss challenges.
- Let children suggest solutions.
- Create simple systems together (chore charts, morning routines).
- Review and adjust approaches based on what's working.

The goal isn't perfect behavior but gradual improvement. When children understand the "why" behind expectations and have tools to meet them, they're more likely to make positive choices.

Practical Implementation

- Start with one challenging situation you face regularly.
- Plan your teaching response in advance.
- Share the new approach with your child during a calm moment.
- Be consistent with the new method for at least two weeks.
- Notice and celebrate small improvements.

The shift from punishment to teaching takes more time initially but leads to better long-term results. Children learn problem-solving skills, emotional regulation, and responsibility tools they'll use throughout their lives.

The Positive Moments Treasure Hunt: A Weekly Family Challenge for Building Better Relationships

The purpose of this activity is to help families spot and create opportunities for positive interactions, respectful communication, and constructive discipline throughout the week.

Materials needed:

- a "Treasure Map" (a simple weekly chart)
- small stickers or markers
- a jar or box for collecting "treasure tickets"
- small pieces of paper for writing treasure tickets

How it works:

Create a colorful chart with these daily "treasure spots" to find

- a moment when someone showed respect
- a time someone fixed a mistake in a positive way
- an instance of good listening
- a situation where someone expressed feelings calmly

A MOMENT OF SHOWING UNDERSTANDING FOR OTHERS

When family members spot these moments, they write them on small "treasure tickets" with:

- what happened
- how it made people feel
- what made it special

Example: "Today Jack was upset about losing his game, but instead of throwing the controller, he took deep breaths and said 'I need a break.' Good job handling big feelings!"

DAILY TREASURE SHARE

During dinner or bedtime, family members can

- share their treasure tickets.
- add stickers to the treasure map.
- discuss what made these moments special.
- plan how to create more positive moments tomorrow.

WEEKLY CELEBRATION

At the end of the week

- read all treasure tickets together.
- celebrate the positive moments.
- choose favorite moments to act out.
- plan next week's positive goals.

Tips for Success

- Keep it light and playful.
- Focus on catching good moments rather than pointing out mistakes.
- Make sure everyone gets recognized.
- Include both big and small positive moments.
- Celebrate progress, not perfection.

This activity turns abstract concepts like respect and positive discipline into concrete, observable actions that families can celebrate together. It also helps children internalize good behaviors by making them more visible and rewarding.

Teaching-First Discipline: A Journey of Family Growth

Real Family Journeys: Before and After Case Studies

CASE STUDY 1: THE RUSHING RUNNER

Before: Maya races down the school hallway, knocking over a vase. Her teacher immediately scolds her, assigns detention, and makes her miss recess to think about being more careful.

After: Maya races down the hallway, knocking over a vase. Mrs. Rodriguez reacts by

- inviting Maya to sit and talk calmly.
- acknowledging her excitement about science.
- guiding her to find safer solutions.
- helping her plan better ways to move through the halls.
- engaging her in problem-solving about backpack placement.

Key changes:

- shifted from punishment to problem-solving
- maintained the excitement for learning
- created practical solutions together
- built trust instead of fear

CASE STUDY 2: THE HOMEWORK STRUGGLE

Before: Tom throws his math worksheet across the room in frustration.

- Parent immediately sends him to his room.
- They remove screen privileges for the week.
- They lecture about responsibility.
- He feels more tension and become more resistant.

After: Tom throws his math worksheet in frustration.

- His parent waits for his emotions to settle.
- His parent sit down with him and asks if he is finding maths tough today.
- His parent helps him break down the worksheet into smaller chunks.
- The parent creates a reward for completing each section.
- Tom and his parents plan the homework schedule together.

The evolution:

- Month 1: Required constant parent support.
- Month 3: Tom starts using checklist independently.
- Month 6: Homework battles decrease by 80%.

CASE STUDY 3: THE SIBLING RIVALRY

Before: Sarah takes her brother's toy car without asking.

- immediate punishment: "Go to your room!"
- toys confiscated
- siblings separated without discussion
- pattern repeats next day

After: Sarah takes her brother's toy car without asking.

- Parent facilitates conversation.
- Each child shares their perspective.
- Together they create a toy-sharing schedule.
- The child practices asking nicely for toys.
- They celebrate successful sharing moments.

Progress timeline:

- Week 1: need constant reminders
- Week 4: start using "May I please..."
- Week 8: independently working out toy turns

Building Better Behaviors: The Teaching Approach

Daily Opportunities for Growth

MORNING RUSH

Traditional response:

- yelling about being late
- threats about losing privileges
- everyone starts day stressed

Teaching approach:

- Create visual schedule together.
- Pack bags night before.
- Set up "ready rewards".
- Practice calm morning voice.
- Celebrate smooth mornings.

MEALTIME CHALLENGES

Old pattern:

- forced cleaning of plate
- battles over vegetables
- tension at every meal

New pattern:

- Involve kids in meal planning.
- Create "try it" bites.
- Share favorite food stories.
- Make food exploration fun.
- Notice and praise healthy choices.

The Family Growth Tracker

Week 1: Baseline

Document current challenges:

- frequency of conflicts
- common triggers
- typical responses

Week 4: Early Changes

Track improvements:

- new solutions tried
- successful moments
- areas still challenging

Week 12: Sustained Growth

Celebrate progress:

- reduced conflict frequency
- new skills learned
- positive patterns established

Making It Work: Practical Tips

Start Small

Choose one situation to transform:

- document current approach
- plan teaching response
- practice new method
- track progress
- adjust as needed

Create Support Systems

- family meeting routines
- calm-down corner
- visual reminders
- celebration rituals
- progress charts

The Positive Moments Treasure Hunt

Daily Treasures to Find

- peaceful problem-solving
- kind words used
- helpful actions
- calm responses to frustration
- good listening moments

Weekly Celebration Ideas

- Share favorite moments.
- Act out best solutions.
- Create family awards.
- Plan next week's focus.
- Choose new skills to learn.

Remember

- Change takes time.
- Progress isn't linear.
- Small steps matter.
- Celebrate attempts.
- Keep practicing together.

The journey from punishment to teaching transforms not just behavior but relationships. Each positive interaction builds trust, understanding, and lifelong skills for managing emotions and solving problems.

Key Takeaways

- ❑ Taking a "teaching-first" approach to discipline means viewing misbehavior as a skill gap to address rather than something to punish, helping children develop problem-solving skills and emotional regulation.
- ❑ Specific, descriptive praise ("I noticed how you asked before using your sister's art supplies") is more effective than generic praise ("good job") because it clearly communicates which behaviors are valued.
- ❑ Engaging children in collaborative problem-solving like asking "What could we do differently next time?" or creating solutions together builds their sense of agency and responsibility.

Chapter Five

BUILDING A NEW FAMILY LEGACY

Sometimes the smallest things stick. Like how my kids know exactly which pillows go where for our Sunday circles. Lily grabs the faded blue one her gran gave her. Pete always wants the firm couch cushions.

I started this after Mom died. It wasn't some grand plan; I just couldn't bear how quiet the house had gotten. One Sunday, I pulled everything off the couch and sat my family down with Mom's old brass bell from her classroom. "Just talk to me," I said.

Now it's our thing. Every week, we circle up. The bell passes around, and whoever holds it gets to speak. No fixing, no advice, just listening. Pete told us about failing calculus here. Lily shared her first heartbreak. Jim, my husband, even cried once about missing his dad.

The dog's part of it, too. Labs know things, I swear. Buck always settles right in the middle, like he's holding court.

"This is weird," Pete said once, back in high school. "None of my friends do this."

However, last month when his roommate's mother got sick, guess who suggested they all sit in a circle and talk?

Fostering Growth Through Family Traditions

The beauty of family traditions lies in their simplicity. They don't need to be elaborate or expensive; they're just those regular moments that bring everyone together and make life feel a bit more grounded. Think about your own childhood memories. Often, the ones that stick aren't from big events or expensive trips, but from simple routines like Sunday dinners or bedtime stories that happened day after day.

Making Time for Each Other

Making time for each other might look different for every family, but it's those consistent moments that matter most. Maybe it's pizza and movies on Friday nights, or everyone gathering in the kitchen to make breakfast on weekends. These routines give kids something stable to count on when everything else feels unpredictable. There's something deeply comforting about knowing that no matter what kind of day you've had, you'll all be together at dinner, sharing stories and catching up. These moments create a safe space where everyone can just be themselves.

Evolving Traditions

As families grow and change, their traditions need to evolve too. That bedtime story ritual might naturally transform into late-night chats with your teenager about their day. Saturday morning cartoons could become marathon sessions of picking shows everyone can enjoy. The key isn't sticking rigidly to the same activities, It's more about maintaining that sense of connection while letting the tradition itself change with your family's needs and interests.

Celebrations

We often save celebrations for major milestones, but there's magic in celebrating the small victories too. Your child finally mastering that tough math problem or learning to make breakfast independently, these moments deserve recognition. It doesn't have to be anything grand; sometimes a high five, a special dessert, or even just a note saying "I saw how hard you worked on that" can make all the difference. These small acknowledgments build confidence and show family members that their efforts matter.

Gratitude

In our fast-paced world, it's easy to forget to pause and appreciate what we have. Taking time during natural breaks, maybe at the start of each season or during holidays, to reflect together can become a meaningful tradition of its own. This might mean keeping a family journal, creating photo albums together, or simply chatting over hot chocolate about favorite memories from recent months. These moments of reflection help everyone appreciate their shared history and look forward to creating new memories together.

The most successful family traditions are often the ones that develop naturally and feel authentic to who you are as a family. They might start by accident, like always having ice cream after good news or sharing jokes at breakfast, but they gradually become part of your family's unique story. The key is keeping things simple and flexible enough to adapt as your family grows and changes. Some traditions might fade away, while others take their place. What matters most is that these shared moments, whatever form they take, help weave together the fabric of your family life.

Building Emotional Intelligence: A Family Guide

Core Practices for Emotional Learning

EXPANDING EMOTIONAL VOCABULARY

Help children move beyond basic "happy" or "sad" labels by:

- introducing nuanced feeling words during natural moments
- drawing emotion faces together
- discussing characters' feelings in stories
- making connections between body sensations and emotions

MODELING EMOTIONAL INTELLIGENCE

Children learn by watching us handle

- daily frustrations ("Taking a deep breath helps me think better").
- disappointments ("Let's find another way").
- problem-solving ("I need a minute to calm down before we discuss this").

MAKING IT PART OF DAILY LIFE

Weave emotional learning into regular routines:

- Share feelings during dinner conversations.
- Use a feelings chart on the refrigerator.
- Create a cozy calm-down space.
- Notice and name emotions during play.

The Family Memory Box: A Simple Way to Share Feelings and Celebrate Together

This activity helps families talk about emotions naturally while creating lasting memories. It's flexible enough for all ages and grows with your family.

The basic setup:

- Find any box or container.
- Gather basic art supplies (paper, markers, stickers).
- Pick a regular monthly sharing time that works for everyone.
- Keep it in an easy-to-reach spot.

Adding Memories (The Easy Part)

Throughout the month, family members can put into the container

- quick notes about happy moments
- simple drawings about how they felt
- photos of daily life
- small keepsakes that tell a story
- notes about challenges they faced and overcame

For younger kids, make it visual. They can draw faces showing how they felt or use stickers. Older kids might write short journal entries or save text messages that meant a lot to them.

Monthly Share Time

Make it cozy by gathering in a comfortable spot and take turns sharing:

- Pull one item at a time from the box.
- Let each person tell their story.
- Use simple prompts like:
    - "How did that moment make you feel?"
    - "What helped you feel better?"
    - "Who helped you during this time?"

Keep It Growing

- Save special items in a yearly collection.
- Take a quick family photo each month.
- Let the activity change as your kids grow.
- Add new ways to share that match your family's interests.

Sample sharing moment:

"Look, here's the drawing Emma made when she was nervous about her first day of school. Emma, can you tell us about it? What helped you feel brave that day?"

There's no wrong way to do this. Some months might have lots of items, others just a few. The goal is simply to make space for sharing feelings and memories together.

Making it work for different ages:

- **Little ones (2-5):** Draw pictures, add stickers.
- **School age (6-12):** Write notes, save small mementos.
- **Teens:** Add photos, text messages, achievement screenshots.

Focus on creating a judgment-free space where everyone feels comfortable sharing both happy moments and tough times. This helps build emotional vocabulary naturally through real experiences.

Exploring Family Rituals: A Guided Journal Experience

Family rituals and traditions are the threads that weave our shared stories together, creating lasting bonds and meaningful memories. This journal activity invites you to explore, reflect on, and create intentional family traditions that strengthen your connections.

Reflection Prompts

CURRENT FAMILY RITUALS

Take a moment to reflect on your existing family traditions. Consider both daily routines and special occasions.

1. What daily or weekly rituals currently bring your family together? Think about:

    - morning routines
    - mealtimes
    - bedtime practices
    - weekend activities

Write about a simple family ritual that you cherish and explain why it matters to you.

CHILDHOOD MEMORIES

2. Think back to your own childhood:

    - Which family traditions do you remember most vividly?
    - What feelings do these memories evoke?
    - Which traditions would you like to pass on to future generations?

Describe a childhood tradition that shaped your understanding of family.

CREATING NEW TRADITIONS

3. Imagine new possibilities for family connection:

    - What values would you like your family traditions to reflect?
    - How might you incorporate elements from different family members' cultural backgrounds?
    - What new ritual could you start this week?

Design a new family tradition that combines meaningful elements from your past with your hopes for the future.

SEASONAL AND SPECIAL OCCASIONS

4. Consider how your family marks important moments:

    - How do you celebrate achievements?
    - What makes holidays special in your family?
    - How do you support each other during challenging times?

Write about a celebration or ceremony you'd like to develop or enhance.

INVOLVING EVERYONE

5. Think about ways to include all family members:

    - How can each person contribute to family traditions?
    - What roles could different generations play?
    - How might you accommodate varying schedules and preferences?

Describe how you could make a current family ritual more inclusive and engaging for everyone.

Action Steps

After reflecting on these prompts, choose one area to focus on:

- Select a current ritual to enhance.
- Design a new tradition to introduce.
- Plan a family meeting to discuss ritual ideas.
- Create a family ritual calendar.
- Document your family traditions through photos, videos, or writing.

Implementation Plan

- What specific ritual will you focus on?
- When will you begin?
- Who needs to be involved in the planning?
- What resources or preparations are needed?
- How will you document and preserve this tradition?

Monthly Check-In Questions

Return to these questions each month to reflect on your family's ritual journey:

- What new traditions have you tried?
- How have family members responded?
- What challenges have you encountered?
- What unexpected joys have you discovered?
- What adjustments would make your rituals more meaningful?

The most enduring family rituals often grow naturally from genuine connection and shared values. Be patient as new traditions take root, and remain flexible as they evolve to meet your family's changing needs.

Our Family Legacy Plan: Building Traditions Together

- Fill this out when you have 15-20 quiet minutes.
- Write down your first thoughts. You can always change them later.
- Start with just one or two traditions you'd like to try.
- Keep it simple. The best traditions are often the easiest ones.

Favorite Childhood Memories

What family traditions made you happy as a kid? (For example: Sunday pancakes, bedtime stories, holiday games).

_____
_____

What made these moments special?

_____
_____

Weekly Traditions

What simple thing could you do together each week? Think about:

- meals
- games
- outdoor time
- reading
- music
- art

Our ideas:

_____
_____

We'll start with:

_____
_____

When:

_____

Monthly Traditions

What could you do once a month to make memories? Examples:

- family movie night
- park picnics
- game tournaments
- photo sessions
- trying new foods
- craft projects

Our ideas:

_____
_____

We'll start with:

_____
_____

Best time for this:

_____

Yearly Traditions

Special occasions to celebrate: (birthdays, holidays, achievements, etc.)

_____
_____

How we'll make it special:

_____
_____

For Our First New Tradition

What we need:

_____
_____

Who does what:

Parent(s):

_____
_____

Kids:

_____

Others:

_____

_____

How we'll remember: (calendar, phone reminder, etc.)

_____

_____

If we miss a week, we'll:

_____

_____

CHECK-IN QUESTIONS

After trying a new tradition for a month, ask:

❑ Is everyone enjoying it?

❑ Is it easy enough to keep doing?

❑ Should we adjust anything?

❑ What's working best?

Future Ideas

Keep a running list of traditions you might want to try later.

Quick Tips for Success

- Keep it simple.
- Be flexible: Traditions can change as kids grow.
- Take pictures sometimes.
- Don't worry if you miss occasionally.
- Let kids help plan.
- Have fun with it!

Remember

❑ Start small with one tradition.

❑ Talk about it with your family.

❑ Give it time to become a habit.

❑ Adjust as needed.

❑ Date we started: _____

Family members involved:

_____

_____

Keep this worksheet where you can find it easily. Come back to it when you want to add new traditions or adjust current ones.

Key Takeaways

❑ Simple, consistent family traditions like weekly "Sunday circles" or monthly memory box sharing create safe spaces for authentic connection and emotional expression that children carry into adulthood.

❑ The most meaningful family rituals often emerge naturally and evolve over time, adapting to changing family needs while maintaining the core purpose of bringing everyone together.

❑ Family traditions don't need to be elaborate or expensive to be effective; small, regular moments like sharing meals, bedtime routines, or weekly check-ins provide stability and predictability that children rely on.

❑ Intentionally documenting and celebrating both everyday moments and special occasions helps family members develop emotional intelligence, gratitude, and a shared sense of identity and belonging.

Conclusion

When you first opened this book, perhaps you were looking for answers. Maybe you found yourself reacting to your children in ways that felt painfully familiar—echoes of your own childhood that you promised yourself you'd never repeat. Or perhaps you were simply curious about why we parent the way we do, wondering how to build stronger connections with your children while healing parts of yourself along the way.

Throughout these pages, we've explored the intricate dance between past and present—how our childhood experiences shape our parenting instincts, and how those instincts can be gently reshaped through awareness and intention.

Now, as we prepare to close this chapter of your journey, let's take a moment to gather the insights you've gained and look ahead to the path that continues to unfold. This book can be a companion on your ongoing journey of growth and transformation as a parent.

Core Insights for Your Journey

- Recognize inherited patterns and automatic responses.
- Practice mindful pauses before reacting.
- Embrace imperfection as part of growth.
- Model self-awareness and repair after mistakes.
- Create new family narratives through conscious choices.
- Value small changes that lead to transformation.
- Understand that awareness itself is progress.
- Build emotional safety through consistent presence.
- Honor the past while choosing new paths forward.
- Trust in the ripple effect of conscious parenting.

The Quiet Revolution of Conscious Parenting

Throughout this journey, we've explored how childhood experiences echo through generations, shaping our parenting in ways both subtle and profound. Like well-worn paths in a forest, these patterns can feel inevitable, carved deep by years of repetition.

Yet, each day brings fresh opportunities to forge new trails, to respond with intention rather than reaction, to write new chapters in your family's story.

The Power of Small Changes

Remember those moments when you caught yourself about to repeat an old pattern? When you chose understanding over judgment, presence over perfection, connection over control? These may have felt like small victories, barely worth noting. Yet, these quiet choices are the foundation of lasting change.

Your children witness this journey. They see you wrestling with old habits, striving to respond differently, picking yourself up after difficult moments. In your efforts to grow, you're teaching them something invaluable: that patterns can be broken, that growth is always possible, that love can find new ways to express itself.

Beyond Perfect Parenting

If there's one truth to carry forward, it's this: Exceptional parenting isn't about flawless execution. It's about staying present, remaining curious, and growing alongside your children. It's understanding that some days will find you falling back into old patterns, and trusting that tomorrow brings another opportunity to choose differently.

This journey isn't just about raising children—it's about raising future parents. In your conscious choices, your willingness to examine inherited patterns and choose new responses, you're creating ripples of change that will touch families beyond your own. This is how healing moves through generations: one parent, one choice, one moment at a time.

Beyond Perfect Parenting

If there's one truth to carry forward, it's this: Exceptional parenting isn't about flawless execution. It's about staying present, remaining curious, and growing alongside your children. It's understanding that some days will find you falling back into old patterns, and trusting that tomorrow brings another opportunity to choose differently.

This journey isn't just about raising children—it's about raising future parents. In your conscious choices, your willingness to examine inherited patterns and choose new responses, you're creating ripples of change that will touch families beyond your own. This is how healing moves through generations: one parent, one choice, one moment at a time.

The Path Forward

Your awareness is already changing your family's story. Each time you:

- notice an old pattern trying to emerge
- take that crucial pause before responding
- choose understanding over judgment
- repair a moment that didn't go as planned
- show that emotions are welcome in your home
- model growth and self-reflection

You're already parenting differently. You're showing that while we can't change the past, we can shape the future through our present choices.

A Gentle Reminder

As you continue this journey, be gentle with yourself. Transformation happens gradually, in quiet moments and small choices. There will be days when old patterns feel overwhelming, when progress seems distant. On those days, remember: awareness itself is change. Every noticed pattern, every thoughtful pause, every repair after a difficult moment—these are the building blocks of transformation.

You're writing new lines in your family's story. Write them with courage, with hope, and with the knowledge that every step forward, no matter how small, ripples outward in ways you may never see. This is how healing happens: one conscious choice at a time, one generation after another, creating a legacy of love that grows stronger with each passing day.

Book Five

Introduction

In our increasingly interconnected world, social competence has become as crucial as academic achievement. The ability to forge meaningful connections, navigate complex social situations, and build lasting relationships will shape your child's success in school, career, and life. As parents, we have a unique opportunity to nurture these essential skills during the critical developmental window between ages three and 12.

Building Blocks of Social Development

During these formative years, children are natural learners, absorbing social cues and patterns from every interaction. Each shared toy in preschool, each group project in elementary school, becomes a stepping stone toward lasting social competence. The good news is that supporting this development doesn't require specialized programs or extensive interventions. It happens through mindful guidance in everyday moments.

Core Social Competencies

Empathy: The Heart of Connection

Empathy forms the foundation of meaningful relationships. Watch for those precious moments when your child notices another's feelings, a toddler sharing their favorite toy with a crying friend, or an older child including someone who's feeling left out. These instances signal growing emotional intelligence that will serve them throughout life.

Communication: Finding Their Voice

Strong communication skills empower children to express themselves and understand others. Help them develop these skills through everyday practice—from joining playground conversations to participating in family discussions. When children communicate confidently, they're better equipped to participate in class, form friendships, and advocate for themselves.

Resilience: Bouncing Back

Social interactions inevitably include disappointments from unreciprocated friendship attempts to party invitations that never arrive. Teaching children to handle these setbacks helps build emotional resilience. They learn that challenges are temporary and that they have the inner strength to try again.

Gratitude: The Social Glue

Children who recognize and appreciate kindness develop a positive outlook that naturally draws others to them. Foster gratitude through simple daily practices, like sharing positive moments at dinner or writing thoughtful thank-you notes.

Individual Paths to Social Success

Remember that social development isn't one-size-fits-all. Some children thrive in large groups, while others prefer intimate friendships. Some lead naturally, while others contribute best in supporting roles. The goal isn't personality transformation but helping each child develop authentic social competence.

Navigating the Digital Landscape

Today's social landscape includes both digital and face-to-face interactions. Guide children in developing healthy online communication habits while emphasizing the irreplaceable value of in-person connections. This balanced approach prepares them for our hybrid social world.

The Long-Term Impact

Strong social skills correlate with academic success, career advancement, and relationship satisfaction. Children who navigate social situations effectively are better prepared for teamwork, conflict resolution, and adapting to new environments, which are essential capabilities in today's world.

The Parent's Role

As parents and educators, we teach social skills both directly and by example. Children learn from watching how we handle our own social challenges, make apologies, and

and maintain relationships through difficulties. Create opportunities for social practice through playdates, team activities, and family gatherings where children can build confidence in a supportive environment.

A Continuing Journey

Remember that social development progresses at its own pace, with advances and occasional setbacks. Maintain an encouraging environment where children feel safe to practice and learn from their experiences. Through patient guidance and real-world practice, we can help our children develop the social capabilities they need to thrive in today's interconnected world.

The investment we make in nurturing our children's social skills today will shape not just their futures, but the quality of their daily lives. Every small moment of guidance, every opportunity for practice, contributes to their growing social competence and their ability to build meaningful connections throughout their lives.

Chapter One

THE FOUNDATIONS OF SOCIAL SUCCESS

Six-year-old Emma sits at the edge of the playground during recess, watching other children play tag and climb on the jungle gym. Her teacher notices that this isn't just a one-time occurrence; day after day, Emma chooses to observe rather than participate. At home, her parents have noticed she's becoming increasingly reluctant to attend birthday parties or playdates. While some children naturally take longer to warm up to social situations, Emma's behavior has both her parents and teacher wondering how they can help her feel more confident in connecting with her peers.

Emma's story is one that many parents and educators will find familiar. Social challenges in children often show up in quiet ways. They may hesitate to join group activities, have difficulty maintaining conversations with peers, or have anxiety about social situations. These aren't just passing phases; they're important signals that a child might need extra support in developing their social skills.

Understanding and addressing these early signs is crucial for children's long-term social success. Just as we teach children to read and write, we need to guide them in developing the social tools they'll use throughout their lives. This involves creating environments where children feel safe to practice these skills, whether at home or in school.

Think of social skills as building blocks. Each positive interaction, each successful navigation of a social situation, adds another block to the foundation. When parents and teachers work together, sharing observations and strategies, they create a strong support system that helps children like Emma develop the confidence to step off the sidelines and into meaningful friendships and social interactions.

Let's explore how we can help children build these essential social skills, one step at a time. Whether you're a parent concerned about your child's social development or an educator looking to support students in your classroom, this chapter will provide practical strategies for fostering social growth and confidence in children of all ages.

The journey toward social confidence isn't always straightforward, but with understanding, patience, and the right tools, we can help every child find their place in the social world. After all, today's playground interactions are tomorrow's life skills, shaping how our children will connect with others throughout their lives.

Recognizing and Supporting Socially Struggling Kids

When children struggle with social connections, hanging back at playgrounds or becoming withdrawn at group events, early, gentle support can make a significant difference. Like teaching any skill, helping children build social confidence works best when we break it down into manageable steps.

Start with your home environment as a safe practice space. Board games teach turn-taking and handling competition, while small playdates with one or two friends allow your child to develop friendship skills with support nearby. These controlled situations help build confidence before tackling larger social settings.

Create a support network by partnering with teachers. They observe your child in different social contexts and can provide valuable insights about both challenges and successes. This collaboration helps ensure consistent support across home and school environments.

Most importantly, focus on gradual progress rather than immediate transformation. Some children may need structured activities like small playgroups or guidance from social skills specialists, while others might benefit most from quiet encouragement and practice at home. The key is matching the support to your child's specific needs and comfort level.

Modeling Healthy Behaviors for Children

Your kids are always watching and learning from you, even when you think they're not paying attention! The way you talk to others, handle tough situations, and show understanding becomes their blueprint for how to behave with others. As their first and most important teacher when it comes to people skills, your everyday actions shape how they'll interact with others throughout their lives.

When it comes to being understanding, small moments make a big difference. When your child comes home upset about something that happened at school, taking time to listen and saying things like "That does sound frustrating" shows them how to care about others' feelings. This simple act teaches them to be a better friend, who can understand when their classmates are having a tough day. They learn that feelings matter and that showing empathy helps build stronger relationships.

The way you communicate with others creates lasting impressions on your children. Whether you're chatting with the grocery store cashier, talking to your partner, or handling a phone call, your children are picking up cues about how to interact with others. When they see you listening without interrupting and speaking kindly, they'll likely mirror these behaviors in their own friendships. These everyday interactions become their guide for how to talk to others respectfully.

Handling disagreements constructively is another crucial lesson children learn from watching their parents. Instead of yelling when something goes wrong, showing your kids how to calmly work through problems makes a big impression. For example, when there's a misunderstanding with a neighbor, talking it out respectfully teaches your kids valuable skills for handling arguments with their friends. They learn that conflicts can be resolved peacefully and that finding solutions together is better than fighting.

Your attitude toward social situations significantly influences your children's confidence in meeting new people. When you're genuinely happy to meet new people or join in community activities, your kids are more likely to feel confident doing the same. Even something as simple as chatting warmly with other parents at the park shows your kids that meeting new people can be enjoyable and rewarding. This positive outlook helps them approach social situations with optimism rather than anxiety.

Creating a supportive home environment is essential for developing these social skills. Having regular family talks where everyone gets a chance to share their thoughts, including your kids in some family decisions like planning weekend activities, and giving them your full attention when they tell you about their day all contribute to building their social confidence. These practices show them that their thoughts and feelings are valued, which helps them feel more secure in expressing themselves with others.

Working with your child's teachers adds another valuable layer of support. Regular communication through quick chats at pickup time or during parent-teacher meetings helps you understand how your child is doing with friends at school. This partnership ensures that both home and school environments support your child's social development consistently. Teachers can offer insights into your child's social interactions that you might not see at home, helping you better support their growth.

Remember that your everyday actions speak louder than words. When you consistently show kindness, respect, and understanding in your own life, you're giving your kids the tools they need to build great friendships of their own. This natural learning process, supported by your positive example and gentle guidance, helps your children develop into socially confident individuals who can build and maintain healthy relationships throughout their lives.

Enhanced Social Skills Development Program

Social Growth Stages Chart

Before diving into weekly activities, use this chart to identify your child's current developmental stage and track their progress:

STAGE 1: FOUNDATION (TYPICALLY AGES 3-4)

Key indicators

- makes eye contact when spoken to
- recognizes basic emotions (happy, sad, angry)
- engages in parallel play
- responds to name
- shows interest in peers

Next steps

- Practice naming emotions.
- Encourage side-by-side play.
- Teach model basic greetings.

STAGE 2: EMERGING SOCIAL AWARENESS (TYPICALLY AGES 4-5)

Key indicators

- initiates simple interactions
- takes turns with prompting
- shows early empathy
- joins group activities with support
- uses basic emotional vocabulary

Next steps

- Practice turn-taking games.
- Role-play social scenarios.
- Encourage asking to join activities.

STAGE 3: ACTIVE SOCIAL ENGAGEMENT (TYPICALLY AGES 5-6)

Key indicators

- maintains brief conversations
- shows genuine concern for others
- negotiates simple conflicts
- initiates play with peers
- understands basic social rules

Next steps

- Practice conflict resolution.
- Develop conversation skills.
- Build friendship-making strategies.

STAGE 4: SOCIAL FLUENCY (TYPICALLY AGES 6-7)

Key indicators

- maintains friendships
- resolves conflicts independently

- shows advanced empathy
- adapts to different social situations
- understands complex emotions

Next steps

- Develop leadership skills.
- Practice group problem-solving.
- Build emotional resilience.

Weekly Themes and Activities

Each activity is now structured with clear progression markers and specific success criteria.

WEEK 1: UNDERSTANDING EMOTIONS

The feelings detective game

Prerequisites: Child should be able to recognize basic facial expressions.

Target stage: foundation to emerging social awareness.

Materials

- full-length mirror
- laminated emotion cards (provided template with 12 core emotions)
- chart paper
- washable markers
- "emotion of the day" tracking sheet

Structured activity steps

1. Morning check-in (5 minutes):

   - Child selects current emotion from card set.
   - Child records on tracking sheet.
   - Child discusses why they feel this way.

2. Emotion exploration (10 minutes):

    ○ Select three emotion cards randomly.
    ○ Practice expressions in mirror.
    ○ Partners guess and provide feedback.
    ○ Document successful identifications.

3. Real-world connection (10 minutes):

    ○ Share personal experience for each emotion.
    ○ Record triggers and coping strategies.
    ○ Create action plan for difficult emotions.

Success indicators

- correctly identifies 8/12 basic emotions
- uses emotion vocabulary unprompted
- shows interest in others' feelings
- begins to link emotions with experiences

WEEK 2: ACTIVE LISTENING

The enhanced echo circle

Prerequisites: basic attention span of 2–3 minutes.

Target stage: emerging social awareness to active social engagement.

Materials

- specialized listening stick with visual cues
- timer
- listening checklist cards
- progress tracking sheets

Structured activity steps

1. Listening preparation (5 minutes):

    ○ Review listening body language.
    ○ Practice "listening pose".
    ○ Set personal listening goal.

2. Structured sharing (15 minutes):

    - Share using specific prompt cards.
    - Use "5 W's" framework.
    - Practice clarifying questions.

3. Active echo practice (10 minutes):

    - Repeat key details.
    - Ask follow-up questions.
    - Demonstrate understanding.

Success indicators

- maintains eye contact for 30+ seconds
- asks relevant follow-up questions
- accurately recalls 3+ key details
- shows visible listening behaviors

[Subsequent weeks following similar detailed structure...]

Implementation Toolkit

FOR PARENTS

Daily practice Framework

1. Morning social skills check-in (5 minutes).

    - review daily social goal
    - practice target skill
    - set intention for the day

2. Structured practice time (20 minutes).

    - follow activity guides
    - document attempts and successes
    - provide specific feedback

3. Evening reflection (10 minutes).

    - review day's interactions
    - celebrate progress
    - plan next day's focus

Progress Monitoring System

Weekly Assessment Tools

1. Social skills tracking sheet.

    - date
    - target skill
    - number of attempts
    - success rate
    - notes on challenges
    - next steps

2. Behavioral frequency chart.

    - Track specific behaviors.
    - Note triggers.
    - Record successful strategies.
    - Document progression.

3. Monthly progress summary.

    - Compare to baseline.
    - Note new skills emerged.
    - Identify areas needing focus.
    - Update action plan.

Parent Reflection and Planning Guide

Weekly reflection questions

1. Skill development.
    - Which skills showed improvement?
    - What new challenges emerged?

○ How did your child respond to different strategies?

2. Environmental factors.

   ○ What settings supported success?
   ○ Which situations proved challenging?
   ○ How can the environment be modified?

3. Support effectiveness.

   ○ Which strategies worked best?
   ○ What adjustments are needed?
   ○ What additional resources would help?

Action planning template

1. Short-term goals (Next 2 weeks).

   ○ target behaviors
   ○ specific strategies
   ○ success metrics

2. Medium-term goals (1-3 months).

   ○ skill progression
   ○ environmental modifications
   ○ support system development

3. Long-term vision (3-6 months).

   ○ desired outcomes
   ○ major milestones
   ○ resource needs

This program has been designed to be flexible and adaptable to your child's unique developmental pace. Use the Social Growth Stages chart as your primary guide, and adjust activities and expectations accordingly. Regular documentation and reflection will help you identify patterns and adjust strategies for optimal support of your child's social development.

Key Takeaways

- Social skills develop in predictable stages (Foundation, Emerging Social Awareness, Active Social Engagement, and Social Fluency), and identifying a child's current stage helps parents and educators provide appropriate support tailored to their developmental needs.
- Parents serve as critical social skills models through their everyday interactions—the way they handle conflicts, show empathy, and engage with others becomes the blueprint children use for their own social relationships.
- Creating structured opportunities for practice through activities like emotion recognition games and active listening exercises helps children build social confidence in manageable steps before facing more challenging social situations.
- Effective social skills development requires consistent collaboration between parents and teachers, along with systematic tracking of progress using tools like behavioral frequency charts and reflection questions to identify patterns and adjust strategies.

Chapter Two

STRATEGIES TO HELP CHILDREN OVERCOME SOCIAL CHALLENGES

Every morning, Alex would stand at the edge of the playground, his hands deep in his pockets, watching the whirlwind of activity before him. He wasn't hiding exactly. He had learned to position himself near the basketball court where he could see everything: the group playing four-square, the jump rope champions, and especially the chess club that met at the picnic tables under the oak tree.

What others might have seen as hesitation was actually Alex's careful study. He noticed how Marcus always made others laugh during four-square, not by being the best player, but by making up silly rules that made everyone giggle. He observed how Sarah, who used to be as quiet as him, had found her place by teaching younger kids how to jump rope. It was the chess club that really caught his attention; the way the players concentrated, celebrated wins, and helped each other learn from losses.

One Tuesday morning, instead of his usual spot by the basketball court, Alex took three careful steps toward the chess tables. He had been practicing with his grandfather every weekend, learning openings and strategies, preparing for this moment. When Danny, the club's unofficial leader, looked up and noticed him, Alex almost retreated. But then Danny smiled and pulled out an empty chair.

"Hey, want to play?" Danny asked, already setting up the pieces. "We need someone new to challenge Carlos—he's won three games in a row."

That simple invitation was all it took. Alex had found his way in, not by forcing himself into the loudest group or trying to be someone he wasn't, but by finding a connection that felt natural to him. By the end of recess, he had played two games (winning one), learned everyone's names, and even helped explain a knight's movement to a curious first-grader who had stopped to watch.

Building Social Confidence: A Structured Approach

The Social Confidence Ladder

Each rung represents progressively more challenging social interactions. Children can move up when they feel comfortable at their current level, or move back down if they need to rebuild confidence.

LEVEL 1: COMFORTABLE OBSERVER

Activities

- Watch other children play from a safe distance.
- Observe social interactions during family gatherings.
- Look at photos of social situations and discuss what's happening.
- Practice social skills with stuffed animals or toys.

Parent support

- Validate the child's desire to watch first.
- Point out positive social interactions they observe.
- Create a "watching spot" where they feel safe observing.
- Use observed situations as teaching moments.

LEVEL 2: NON-VERBAL PARTICIPANT

Activities

- Wave to familiar people.
- Give thumbs up or high-fives.
- Join group activities without speaking (coloring, building).
- Use gestures to communicate needs.
- Smile at peers when making eye contact.

Parent support

- Practice non-verbal greetings at home.
- Create signals for common needs.
- Celebrate each gesture of engagement.
- Model positive body language.

LEVEL 3: PARALLEL PLAYER

Activities

- Play alongside peers without direct interaction.
- Share space during structured activities.
- Participate in group activities with individual roles.
- Follow along with group movement activities.

Parent support

- Arrange side-by-side play opportunities.
- Create structured activities where each child has their own materials.
- Use proximity without pressure to interact.
- Acknowledge comfortable co-existence.

LEVEL 4: SUPPORTED INTERACTOR

Activities

- Respond to direct questions with one-word answers.
- Participate in turn-taking games with adult support.
- Join structured group activities with clear roles.
- Share materials when prompted.

Parent support

- Provide scripted responses for common situations.
- Be present during initial interactions.
- Create structured play scenarios.
- Use prompt cards for social situations.

LEVEL 5: INITIATOR-IN-TRAINING

Activities

- Ask for materials using prepared phrases.
- Invite one familiar peer to play.
- Share simple information about themselves.
- Join ongoing activities using practiced phrases.

Parent support

- Role-play common social scenarios.
- Create social scripts for different situations.
- Practice invitation phrases.
- Build a repertoire of conversation starters.

LEVEL 6: CONFIDENT COMMUNICATOR

Activities

- Start conversations with peers.
- Suggest game ideas to the group.
- Express opinions in small groups.
- Handle simple social challenges independently.

Parent support

- Discuss social problem-solving strategies.
- Practice more complex social scenarios.
- Gradually reduce adult intervention.
- Celebrate independent interactions.

Differentiated Strategies by Personality Type

For the Analytical Child

- Break down social situations into observable patterns.
- Create social "flow charts" for different scenarios.
- Use social skills checklists.
- Track progress with concrete metrics.

For the Creative Child

- Use storytelling to explore social situations.
- Draw pictures of successful social interactions.
- Create social scenarios through pretend play.
- Express feelings through art or music.

For the Physical Child

- Use movement games to build social confidence.
- Practice social skills through sports activities.
- Incorporate action into social learning.
- Use physical space to understand social boundaries.

For the Verbal Child

- Develop scripts for different social situations.
- Practice word choices for various scenarios.
- Use storytelling to explore social solutions.
- Build a vocabulary for expressing feelings.

Implementation Strategies

Daily Practice Opportunities

1. Morning preparation.

    - Review current ladder level.
    - Set specific social goal for the day.
    - Practice relevant skills.
    - Plan for potential challenges.

2. After-school review.

    - Discuss social interactions.
    - Celebrate progress.
    - Identify challenges.
    - Plan next steps.

Weekly Skill Building

- Choose one specific skill to focus on.
- Practice in three different settings.
- Document progress and challenges.
- Adjust strategies as needed.

Progress Tracking

Success Indicators

- increased comfort in social situations
- more frequent social initiations
- longer duration of social interactions
- greater variety of social partners
- more independent problem-solving
- reduced anxiety about social situations

Red Flags

- regression to earlier ladder levels
- increased resistance to social situations
- physical complaints before social events
- avoidance of previously mastered skills

Parent Support Network

Building Your Support System

- Connect with other parents.
- Share strategies and successes.
- Create practice opportunities.
- Exchange resources and ideas.

Professional Support

Consider consulting with:

- school counselor
- social skills group facilitator
- child psychologist
- occupational therapist

The goal isn't to eliminate shyness but to build confidence and competence in social situations. Each child's journey up the Social Confidence Ladder will be unique. Celebrate progress at every level and adjust the pace to match your child's comfort and readiness.

Gradual Exposure: Creating a Social Comfort Ladder

Level 1: One-on-One Interactions

- Start with brief, structured playdates (30-60 minutes) at home.
- Choose activities your child enjoys and excels at.

- Include clear beginning and end times.
- Have a planned activity ready (building sets, art project, favorite game).

Level 2: Small Group Settings

- Host mini-playgroups with two to three familiar peers.
- Join small, structured activities (art class, reading circle).
- Participate in small team sports practices before full games.
- Attend small birthday parties with close friends before larger celebrations.

Level 3: Structured Group Activities

- Join organized clubs with clear roles and expectations.
- Participate in group projects with defined responsibilities.
- Attend community classes with consistent peer groups.
- Engage in team sports or group performances.

Level 4: Larger Social Settings

- Attend larger community events with a small group of familiar friends.
- Participate in school-wide activities with a buddy.
- Join larger gatherings with the option to take breaks.
- Engage in multi-group activities or competitions.

Leadership Development Through Natural Opportunities

AT HOME

- Plan and lead a family game night.
- Teach siblings or younger cousins a skill.
- Create and explain rules for a new game.
- Organize a family cleanup project.

IN SCHOOL

- Take responsibility for classroom tasks.
- Lead small group discussions.
- Present projects to the class.
- Help organize class events.

IN COMMUNITY

- Assist with organizing neighborhood activities.
- Lead warm-up exercises in sports practice.
- Help younger children at community events.
- Take charge of a service project.

Practice Scenarios for Common Social Situations

JOINING ACTIVITIES

- "Can I play with you?"
- "That looks fun—how do you play?"
- "Would it be okay if I joined in?"
- "I know how to play that game. Could I take a turn?"

MAKING NEW FRIENDS

- Introducing yourself to new classmates.
- Starting a conversation about shared interests.
- Asking questions about others' hobbies.
- Inviting someone to play or sit together.

PROBLEM-SOLVING SITUATIONS

- Handling disagreements about game rules.
- Responding to accidental bumps or conflicts.
- Taking turns with popular equipment.
- Dealing with competitive situations.

Real-World Practice Opportunities

STRUCTURED SETTINGS

- library story time
- community center classes
- religious or cultural group activities
- supervised sports practice

SEMI-STRUCTURED ACTIVITIES

- open gym sessions
- park playdates
- community playground visits
- drop-in art classes

NATURAL SOCIAL SITUATIONS

- grocery store interactions
- neighborhood walks
- restaurant ordering
- library book checkouts

Parents as Social Coaches

MODELING SOCIAL SKILLS

- Demonstrate friendly greetings with neighbors.
- Show positive problem-solving with others.
- Handle public interactions with grace.
- Maintain healthy friendships.

SUPPORTING SOCIAL GROWTH

- Observe without hovering.
- Offer gentle prompts when needed.
- Provide specific praise for effort.
- Discuss social situations constructively.

PROCESSING SOCIAL EXPERIENCES

- "What went well today?"
- "What strategies helped you feel comfortable?"
- "What might you try differently next time?"
- "How did others respond when you...?"

Progress Tracking and Celebration

SMALL WINS TO CELEBRATE

- Using a new social phrase successfully.
- taking initiative in a familiar setting
- recovering from a social challenge
- helping another child feel included

GROWTH INDICATORS

- Increased comfort in familiar settings.
- Willingness to try new social situations.
- More frequent positive peer interactions.
- Growing confidence in leadership roles.

The Social Confidence Journey

A 6-Week Activity Program for Building Social Skills

Every child has their own unique way of connecting with others. This program helps children discover their social strengths through gradual, comfortable steps.

MATERIALS NEEDED

- a special notebook (The Confidence Journal)
- colored markers or stickers
- a small whiteboard for practice sessions
- basic board games
- calendar for tracking progress

Week 1: Observation Week

ACTIVITY: THE PEOPLE WATCHING GAME

- Just like Alex watched different playground activities, encourage your child to be a "social scientist".
- Create a fun observation journal.

- Daily task: Notice and write down one interesting thing about how other kids play or interact.
- End-of-week celebration: Draw their favorite observed activity.

Week 2: Finding Your Social Power

ACTIVITY: INTEREST EXPLORER

- Help children identify their special interests (like Alex's chess).
- Create a list of activities they enjoy.
- Practice talking about these interests using the whiteboard.
- Role-play introducing their hobby to someone new.
- Daily challenge: Share one interesting fact about their favorite activity.

Week 3: Small Steps Challenge

ACTIVITY: THE HELLO PROJECT

- Create a "Hello Chart" with different greeting levels:
  - wave from far away
  - smile and wave
  - say "hi" softly
  - say "hello" clearly
  - say "hello" and the person's name
- Daily goal: Try one level they feel comfortable with.
- Track their progress with stickers or drawings.

Week 4: Friendship Skills Workshop

ACTIVITY: THE GOOD FRIEND GAME

- Create situation cards with common social scenarios.
- Practice responses through role-play.
- Topics include
  - asking to join a game
  - taking turns
  - sharing toys
  - giving compliments
  - handling disagreements

- Daily practice: Act out one scenario with a family member.

Week 5: Leadership Moments

ACTIVITY: HELPER HEROES

- Create a list of simple leadership opportunities.
- Examples:
    - Teaching someone a game rule.
    - Showing a new student around.
    - Organizing a small game.
    - Helping set up an activity.
- Weekly goal: Try one helper task.
- Document the experience with drawings or stories.

Week 6: Social Confidence Celebration

ACTIVITY: FRIENDSHIP FESTIVAL

- Plan a small gathering (2-3 friends).
- Let your child
    - choose the activities.
    - help prepare snacks.
    - create simple rules for games.
    - take turns leading different activities.
- Create a "My Social Journey" scrapbook page.

Implementation Tips

FOR PARENTS

- Keep activities light and playful.
- Never force participation.
- Celebrate every small step.
- Share your own social learning stories.
- Document progress with photos or notes.

FOR TEACHERS

- Use activities during free play or circle time.
- Pair children with compatible personalities.
- Create helper roles that match each child's interests.
- Share progress with parents.
- Provide quiet spaces for breaks.

Progress Tracking

Create a "Social Growth Garden":

- Draw a flower with six petals.
- Color one petal for each completed week.
- Write or draw a favorite moment in each petal.
- Display prominently to celebrate progress.

Key Takeaways

❑ Building social confidence works best as a gradual process using a "Social Confidence Ladder" approach, where children progress from comfortable observation to active participation at their own pace.
❑ Children often find social success by connecting through their natural interests and strengths rather than forcing themselves into interactions that don't match their personality.
❑ Effective social skills development should be tailored to different personality types, such as analytical, creative, physical, or verbal with strategies that leverage each child's unique way of understanding and engaging with the world.
❑ Parents and teachers can support social growth through structured opportunities.

Chapter Three

TEACHING EMPATHY AND GRATITUDE

Lilly stood in the doorway of her classroom, clutching her backpack straps tightly. The rain was pouring outside, and she'd forgotten her umbrella again. As she watched other kids rush past with their colorful raincoats and umbrellas, she felt her eyes start to sting with frustrated tears.

Then she noticed Ethan, a quiet boy from her art class, standing nearby. Without saying a word, he pulled out an oversized umbrella from his bag. "Want to share?" he asked simply, remembering how last week Lilly had shared her last cookie with him when he'd dropped his lunch.

As they walked together, taking turns avoiding puddles and giggling when they both jumped over a particularly large one, Lilly felt something shift inside her. She thought about how just yesterday she'd seen Ethan sitting alone at lunch, but hadn't thought much of it. Now, under the shelter of his shared umbrella, she realized sometimes the smallest gestures could feel like the biggest gifts.

The next day, Lilly did something different at lunch. She spotted Ethan at his usual table and walked over with her tray. "Want to share?" she asked, echoing his words from the day before.

Building Empathy and Gratitude: A Family Guide

Interactive Learning Activities

STORY EXPLORATION SESSIONS

- Read together and discuss character emotions.
- Ask questions like "How would you feel in their place?"

- Create alternative endings based on different character choices.
- Draw connections to real-life situations.

FAMILY DISCUSSION RITUALS

- Share daily highlights and challenges at dinner.
- Practice active listening when others speak.
- Express gratitude for specific actions.
- Acknowledge different perspectives on shared experiences.

Role-Playing With Purpose

SCENARIO PRACTICE

- Act out being the new student at school.
- Practice responding to a friend's disappointment.
- Explore different ways to handle conflicts.
- Demonstrate helping someone who's struggling.

EMPATHY-BUILDING GAMES

- A Day in Someone's Shoes: This allows them to experience different life situations.
- Feelings Detective: Children guess emotions from facial expressions.
- What Would You Do?: These depict different situations.
- Gratitude scavenger hunt.

Community Service Projects for Families

Local Impact Initiatives

NEIGHBORHOOD CARE PROGRAM

- Organize a street cleanup day.
- Create welcome packages for new families.
- Start a community garden.
- Help elderly neighbors with yard work.

SCHOOL SUPPORT PROJECTS

- Collect supplies for classrooms.
- Create appreciation cards for school staff.
- Organize playground cleanup days.
- Start a peer tutoring program.

ENVIRONMENTAL STEWARDSHIP

- Adopt a local park or beach.
- Start a neighborhood recycling initiative.
- Plant trees or create butterfly gardens.
- Organize eco-friendly awareness campaigns.

Support for Vulnerable Populations

- Partner with senior centers for visiting programs.
- Collect essentials for homeless shelters.
- Create care packages for hospital patients.
- Support local animal shelters.

Combining Gratitude and Empathy

MORNING APPRECIATION CIRCLE

- Share one thing you're grateful for.
- Acknowledge someone who helped you recently.
- Express understanding for others' challenges.
- Plan one way to help others today.

EVENING REFLECTION TIME

- Discuss acts of kindness witnessed or performed.
- Share moments of connection with others.
- Recognize challenges others faced.
- Plan tomorrow's helpful actions.

Creative Expression Activities

FAMILY GRATITUDE JOURNAL

- Write or draw daily entries.
- Include photos of helping moments.
- Document community service experiences.
- Record different perspectives on shared events.

KINDNESS AND APPRECIATION PROJECTS

- Create thank-you cards for community helpers.
- Make appreciation videos for family members.
- Design posters about understanding others.
- Build a family kindness calendar.

Making It Part of Daily Life

NATURAL LEARNING MOMENTS

- Use media discussions to explore different perspectives.
- Point out real-life examples of empathy in action.
- Celebrate diverse viewpoints during family decisions.
- Notice and acknowledge others' helpful actions.

BUILDING LASTING HABITS

- Start with small, manageable activities.
- Make it fun and age-appropriate.
- Celebrate effort over perfection.
- Connect activities to real-world impact.

Impact and Growth

The combination of practicing gratitude while developing empathy creates a powerful foundation for children's social and emotional growth. When kids regularly exercise both skills, they

- develop stronger relationships.

- handle challenges more effectively.
- show greater resilience.
- demonstrate increased kindness.
- build deeper understanding of others.
- create positive community connections.

These skills develop gradually through consistent practice and example. Each small moment of understanding or appreciation builds toward lasting character development and stronger community connections.

Key Takeaways

❑ Small, reciprocal acts of kindness (like sharing an umbrella or lunch) create meaningful connections between children and teach them that empathy often comes full circle.

❑ Regular family rituals like morning appreciation circles and evening reflection times help children develop the habit of noticing others' needs and expressing gratitude for kindnesses received.

❑ Engaging children in interactive learning activities such as role-playing scenarios, story discussions, and empathy-building games helps them practice understanding different perspectives.

❑ Community service projects that involve the whole family, from neighborhood cleanups to supporting vulnerable populations, provide practical, real-world opportunities for children to develop empathy beyond their immediate social circles.

Chapter Four

MASTERING COMMUNICATION SKILLS

Annie hands twisted nervously in her lap as she sat across from her best friend Emma during recess. Yesterday, they'd argued over who would get to be team captain in gym class, and now the silence between them felt as heavy as their lunch boxes.

"I didn't like how it made me feel when you said I never let you be captain," Emma finally said, her voice quiet but steady, just like their teacher had taught them in their morning circle discussions about expressing feelings.

Annie took a deep breath, remembering Ms. Thompson's lessons about active listening. Instead of jumping to defend herself, she tried to repeat what she'd heard. "So, you felt hurt because you thought I was saying you're not fair?" She watched Emma's face carefully as she spoke., you felt hurt because you thought I was saying you're not fair?" She watched Emma's face carefully as she spoke.

Emma nodded, then added, "But I also understand that you really wanted a turn to lead the team."

The tight knot in Annie's chest began to loosen. She remembered how last week, during their class communication practice, they'd learned about finding solutions together. "Maybe we could take turns?" she suggested. "Like, you could be captain this Wednesday, and I could do it next Monday?"

Emma's face brightened. "That's perfect! And we could even help each other come up with fun team strategies!"

Developing Active Listening and Conflict Resolution

The magic of childhood lies in its boundless imagination. Watch any group of children at play, and you'll witness doctors treating stuffed animal patients with careful attention, teachers guiding imaginary classrooms with authority, or chefs preparing elaborate pretend meals in makeshift kitchens. These moments of imaginative play are far more than simple entertainment—they're powerful opportunities for developing crucial social and emotional skills that will serve children throughout their lives.—they're powerful opportunities for developing crucial social and emotional skills that will serve children throughout their lives.

The Natural Laboratory of Pretend Play

Children instinctively use make-believe scenarios to process and understand their world. When a child pretends to be a shopkeeper carefully counting change, they're not just mimicking adult behaviors—they're practicing patience, precision, and positive interactions. These natural inclinations toward role-play provide parents and educators with an ideal framework for teaching more complex social skills through guided practice.—they're practicing patience, precision, and positive interactions. These natural inclinations toward role-play provide parents and educators with an ideal framework for teaching more complex social skills through guided practice.

Consider the young child who transforms their bedroom into a bustling restaurant. As they take orders from their teddy bear customers, they're unconsciously developing crucial skills: listening attentively, responding appropriately, solving problems as they arise, and adapting their communication style to different situations. Each playful interaction becomes a building block for real-world social competence.

Master Social Skills Role-Play Guide

Getting Started With Role-Play

- Choose a quiet, comfortable space.
- Start with 10-15 minute sessions.
- Keep props simple and minimal.
- Use stuffed animals for reluctant participants.
- Record successful strategies in a notebook.

Core Scenario Categories

Friendship Initiation Scenarios

MAKING FIRST CONTACT

- skills: introduction, self-expression
- set-up: two chairs in a "playground" setting-up: two chairs in a "playground" setting

SCENARIO OPTIONS

1. Approaching a single child..

    - "Hi, I like your toy. What's your name?"
    - "That looks fun. Could you show me how to play?"

2. Joining a group game..

    - "That looks like a fun game. Could I join?"
    - "I know how to play tag. Can I be part of the next round?"

3. Welcoming a new child..

    - "You're new here! Would you like to play with us?"
    - "I can show you where everything is if you'd like."

SUCCESS INDICATORS

- clear voice
- appropriate physical distance
- positive body language
- graceful handling of rejection

Conflict Resolution Scenarios

HANDLING DISAGREEMENTS

- skills: negotiation, emotional regulation

- set-up: relevant props (toys, games, playground equipment)-up: relevant props (toys, games, playground equipment)

Scenario options

1. Sharing resources..

    - two children wanting the same swinging the same swing
    - limited art supplies during a project
    - one computer/tablet for two people

2. Game rule disputes..

    - disagreement about whose turn it is
    - different understandings of rules
    - someone not following agreed rules

3. Personal space issues..

    - someone cutting in line
    - unwanted physical contact
    - too close during circle time

Resolution scripts

- "I understand you want [item]. How about we take turns for five minutes each?"
- "I feel frustrated when [action happens]. Could we find a solution together?"
- "Let's check the rules together to make sure we both understand."

Emotional Expression Scenarios

Managing feelings

- skills: emotional awareness, verbal expression
- set-up: emotion cards, mirrors-up: emotion cards, mirrors

Scenario options

1. Disappointment management..

    - not being chosen for a team
    - losing a game

- friend playing with someone else

2. Excitement control..

    - winning a game
    - special event coming up
    - receiving good news

3. Anxiety navigation..

    - first day of school
    - performance or presentation
    - new social situation

Key phrases

- "I feel [emotion] because [reason]."
- "When I'm [emotion], I can [coping strategy]."
- "It's okay to feel [emotion], but I need to [appropriate action]."

Social Problem-Solving Scenarios

Finding solutions

- skills: critical thinking, compromise
- set-up: problem scenario cards-up: problem scenario cards

Scenario options

1. Group project challenges..

    - partner not participating
    - disagreement about ideas
    - time management issues

2. Friendship dilemmas..

    - friend sharing private information
    - being left out of activities
    - friend pressuring to break rules

3. Classroom situations..

- someone copying work
- disruptive classmate
- understanding teacher's instructions

Problem-solving steps

- Identify the problem.
- Generate possible solutions.
- Consider consequences.
- Choose and implement solution.
- Evaluate results.

Advanced Social Skills Scenarios

Complex interactions

- skills: empathy, perspective-taking
- setup: multiple role-players, scenario cards

Scenario options

1. Leadership situations..

   - organizing a group activity
   - delegating tasks
   - motivating others

2. Cultural awareness..

   - including someone who speaks differently
   - respecting different customs
   - explaining traditions

3. Digital interaction..

   - online game communication
   - group chat etiquette
   - social media kindness

Implementation Tips

For Parents

1. Progressive difficulty..

    - Start with easier scenarios.
    - Gradually increase complexity.
    - Add challenges as confidence grows.

2. Customization strategies..

    - Use child's interests in scenarios.
    - Adapt to current social challenges.
    - Incorporate recent experiences.

3. Practice schedule..

    - two to three times per week
    - 15–20 minutes per session
    - mix different scenario types

Progress Tracking

Weekly assessment

- scenario completion
- comfort level (one to five scale)one to five scale)
- new skills demonstrated
- areas needing practice

Monthly review

- progress patterns
- skill transferal to real situations
- new challenges emerged
- strategy adjustments needed

Celebration and Rewards

Milestone Recognition

- completing new scenario types
- using skills in real situations
- teaching skills to others
- showing consistent progress

Reward Ideas

- special one-on-one time
- choice of next scenario
- leading a practice session
- positive feedback journal

Simple Communication Games

Here are some games you can play with your children to help improve their communication skills.

The Story Chain Game

Start telling a story with just one sentence like "Once there was a purple elephant who loved to dance." Then your child adds the next part, and you keep taking turns. Watch their creativity bloom as they practice listening and building on ideas. This game is perfect for car rides or waiting at restaurants.

Detective Questions

Pick an object in the room but don't tell what it is. Your child gets to ask you questions to figure it out, but you can only answer "yes" or "no." This teaches them how to ask good questions and think carefully about what information they need. "Is it bigger than my shoe?" "Is it something we use every day?"

Mirror, Mirror, Mirror

Stand facing each other and take turns being the leader. The leader makes movements or facial expressions, and the other person copies them exactly. It's silly fun, but it also teaches kids to pay attention to body language and non-verbal communication. You'll both end up laughing while learning!

Feelings Charades

Write down different feelings on small papers: "excited," "tired," "frustrated," "proud." Take turns picking one and acting it out without words. This helps kids recognize emotions and understand how we show feelings without speaking.

The Listening Game

Tell a short story about your day, including specific details. Then ask your child to repeat back three things they remember. Take turns in letting them tell you a story, and you repeat details back. It's amazing how this simple game helps develop active listening skills., and you repeat details back. It's amazing how this simple game helps develop active listening skills.

Back-to-Back Drawing

Sit back-to-back with your child. Give them a blank paper and pencil. You get a simple drawing (like a house with two trees). Describe your picture step by step and have them draw what you describe. Do this without looking at each other's papers. When you're done, compare drawings and laugh about the differences. This really shows how important clear instructions are.

What's different? Look at each other for 30 seconds, then turn around and change one small thing about your appearance. Maybe roll up one sleeve or move your hair to the other side. Turn back and try to spot what's different. This builds observation skills and attention to detail. Look at each other for 30 seconds, then turn around and change one small thing about your appearance. Maybe roll up one sleeve or move your hair to the other side. Turn back and try to spot what's different. This builds observation skills and attention to detail.

The best part about these games is that they don't feel like learning. You can play them anywhere, anytime, and you don't need any special materials. Start with the one that sounds most fun to your child, and don't worry if it gets silly.

If your child gets frustrated, take a break or try a different game. The goal is to build their communication skills while creating happy memories together.

Key Takeaways

- ❑ Children naturally practice important social skills during imaginative play, making role-play an effective framework for teaching more complex social and emotional competencies in a low-pressure environment.
- ❑ Active listening techniques, such as repeating what you've heard and focusing on understanding before responding, help children resolve conflicts constructively.
- ❑ Structured role-play scenarios covering specific social challenges—from friendship initiation to conflict resolution to emotional expression—provide children with practical scripts and strategies they can apply in real-life situations.
- ❑ Simple communication games like Story Chain, Detective Questions, and Back-to-Back Drawing develop crucial listening, questioning, and expression skills while feeling like play rather than instruction.

Chapter Five

PREPARING FOR REAL-WORLD SOCIAL SUCCESS

Marcus stared at his phone, his thumb hovering over the "Share" button. A classmate had posted an embarrassing photo of Katie from math class, and now everyone was sharing it in their group chat. His best friend Alex had already forwarded it, adding laughing emojis and writing "Share this, or you're not cool!"

A knot formed in Marcus's stomach as he remembered last week's family dinner conversation. His older sister had shared her own middle school experience with a similar situation, and how one shared photo had hurt someone's feelings for months. His mom had asked them both, "Before you post or share something, imagine showing it to grandma. Would she be proud of your choice?"

"Hey, did you share it yet?" Alex messaged. "Everyone's waiting!"

Marcus took a deep breath and typed back: "Actually, I don't think we should share that photo. Katie's our classmate, and it might really hurt her feelings." His heart pounded as he hit send.

A moment later, his phone buzzed again. To his surprise, Alex replied, "You know what? You're right. I'm going to delete it from my story." Soon, another classmate chimed in: "Yeah, I wouldn't want someone sharing an embarrassing photo of me either."

That evening, as Marcus helped his mom make dinner, he told her about what happened. "You know," he said, measuring pasta into the pot, "it's kind of like what you always say about being the first penguin to jump in the water. Sometimes you just have to take that first step, even when it's scary."

His mom smiled, remembering how they'd watched that nature documentary together. "And what happened when that first penguin jumped?"

"The others followed," Marcus grinned, realizing that standing up for what's right often just needs someone brave enough to go first.

Building Digital-Social Balance: A Family Framework

Section 1: Device Usage Guidelines

Screen-Free Zones

Our family agrees to the following guidelines for healthy digital habits:

- ☐ bedrooms after __ PM
- ☐ dining room during meals
- ☐ bathrooms
- ☐ family room during family time
- ☐ other: _____

SCREEN FREE TIMES

- ☐ before __ AM
- ☐ during homework (unless needed)
- ☐ family meals
- ☐ one hour before bedtime
- ☐ family outings
- ☐ other: _____

PARENT COMMITMENTS

☐ Set up parental controls.

☐ Review online connections.

☐ Be available for questions.

☐ Model good habits.

☐ Respect privacy within safety limits.

☐ Other: _____

CHILD COMMITMENTS

☐ no sharing personal info without permission

☐ telling parents about uncomfortable situations

☐ asking before downloading/creating accounts

☐ following time limits

☐ using devices in common areas

☐ other: _____

WEEKDAYS

- fun: __ hours/day
- school: __ hours/day
- family chat: __ hours/day

WEEKENDS

- fun: __ hours/day
- school: __ hours/day
- family chat: __ hours/day

TO EARN SCREEN TIME

☐ finishing homework

☐ exercising __ minutes

☐ doing chores

☐ having face-to-face social time

☐ other: _____

REDUCED SCREEN TIME, IF

☐ grades drop

☐ rules broken

☐ chores neglected

☐ contract violated

☐ other: _____

SIGNATURES

Parent: _____ Date: ___

Child: _____ Date: ___

Review date: _____

DAILY LOG

Morning:

- waking up: ___
- first device check: ___
- in-person talks: ___

After school:

- school screen time: ___
- social media: ___
- games: ___
- exercise: ___

Evening:

- family time (no devices): ___
- last screen: ___
- bedtime: ___

Rewards

SHORT-TERM

☐ extra weekend screen time

☐ pick family activity

☐ one-on-one time

☐ new app/game

LONG-TERM

☐ family trip

☐ new privileges

☐ special celebration

☐ tech upgrade

Balancing Digital and Real-World Connections

Just as we guide our children toward balanced nutrition, we need to help them develop a healthy mix of digital and face-to-face interactions. While digital connections offer their own benefits, in-person social experiences provide irreplaceable opportunities for developing emotional intelligence, reading non-verbal cues, and building deep relationships.

Creating Meaningful Family Rhythms

DEVICE-FREE ZONES

Establish protected spaces for family connection, such as:

- meal times for sharing stories and practicing conversation skills.
- morning routines that start with human connection.
- bedtime rituals focused on family bonding.
- weekend morning activities without screens.

STRUCTURED SOCIAL OPPORTUNITIES

Build regular social experiences into family life through:

- scheduled playdates that encourage face-to-face interaction.
- family game nights that develop turn-taking and communication.
- community activities that expand social circles.
- team sports or group classes that teach collaboration.

Digital Citizenship and Real-World Social Skills

TEACHING PARALLEL SKILLS

Help children understand how social skills translate across environments:

- respect for others (both online and offline).
- understanding appropriate sharing boundaries.
- recognizing and responding to others' emotions.
- building and maintaining friendships.

SAFETY AND ETIQUETTE

Guide children in navigating both digital and physical social spaces:

- setting healthy boundaries.
- protecting personal information.
- understanding different types of relationships.
- recognizing when to seek adult help.

Building a Balanced Activity Portfolio

ACTIVE ENGAGEMENT

Encourage activities that develop real-world social skills:

- sports teams and physical activities
- arts and craft classes
- community service projects
- school clubs and organizations.

DIGITAL INTEGRATION

Create purposeful uses of technology:

- family video calls with distant relatives
- educational games that encourage problem-solving
- creative digital projects
- structured online learning experiences.

Implementation Strategies

DAILY PRACTICES

- Set clear expectations for device use.
- Plan regular outdoor activities.
- Schedule face-to-face social time.
- Create opportunities for unstructured play.

FAMILY AGREEMENTS

- Establish shared rules about screen time.
- Define technology-free zones and times.
- Create consequences and rewards that make sense.
- Review and adjust guidelines as children grow.

Moving Forward

Remember that balance looks different for every family. The key is creating rhythms that work for your household while ensuring children develop strong social skills in both digital and physical spaces. Regular check-ins and adjustments help maintain this balance as your children grow and their social needs evolve.

Family Activities That Can Help Build Social Skills

Here are some examples of family activities that can help your children build social skills.

Family Game Nights

Instead of just playing to win, board games become chances to practice taking turns, handling disappointment, and celebrating others' success. Games like Pictionary or Charades help kids read body language and express themselves. Even when someone gets frustrated about losing, it's a perfect moment to talk about managing emotions in a safe, loving environment.

Kitchen Team Work

Cooking together is magical for building cooperation skills. Maybe your younger child helps measure ingredients while the older one reads the recipe. It's about listening to instructions, working as a team, and feeling proud of creating something together. Those dinner conversations while enjoying your creation are also golden opportunities for sharing stories and practicing conversation skills.

"Reporter for a Day"

Take turns being family reporters during car rides or dinner. Each person shares their day's story, while others practice being good listeners by asking questions. "What was the most surprising part?" "How did that make you feel?" This helps kids learn to share stories, ask thoughtful questions, and show interest in others' experiences.

Family Project Planning

Whether you're planning a weekend activity or reorganizing a room, involve everyone in the decision-making. Maybe you're choosing a vacation spot or deciding how to celebrate grandma's birthday. These discussions teach kids how to share ideas, consider others' preferences, and find solutions that work for everyone.

"Kindness Missions"

Make helping others a family adventure. Bake cookies for new neighbors, create care packages for relatives, or clean up a local park together. These activities show kids how good it feels to think about others and work together for a positive purpose.

Role-Play Real Life

Turn everyday challenges into playful practice sessions. If your child is nervous about an upcoming event act it out at home first. Make it fun and silly, and watch their confidence grow.

Nature Walks With a Twist

Turn regular walks into observation games. "What do you notice that's different today?" "Can you spot something that makes you curious?" This builds observation skills and teaches kids to pay attention to their surroundings.

Creative Storytelling

Start a story and have each family member add to it. This teaches kids to listen carefully, build on others' ideas, and express themselves creatively.

Weekend "Unplugged" Time

Set aside times when everyone unplugs from devices. Use this time to build puzzles together, do art projects, or just hang out and chat. It shows kids that real-life connections can be more fun than screen time.

Sometimes the best learning happens during the messy moments like when someone gets frustrated, when plans don't work out exactly right, or when we have to figure out compromises together. These are all growth opportunities.

Creating Your Family's Social Calendar: Finding Joy in the Balance

Balancing your family's social life can feel like juggling while riding a unicycle. Between school activities, sports practices, family obligations, and those precious moments of downtime, finding the right mix takes some creativity. With a little planning (and a lot of flexibility), you can create a social calendar that enriches your children's lives without overwhelming your family.

Starting With the Basics

Think of your family's social calendar like a pizza; you want a good base before adding all the toppings.

Start with your non-negotiables:

- school hours and homework time
- parents' work schedules
- essential appointments and commitments
- bedtimes and morning routines

These create the framework around which you'll build your social activities.

The "Just Right" Mix

WEEKLY RHYTHM

Picture a typical week that feels good for your family. It might look something like this:

- **Monday:** low-key afternoon at home after school
- **Tuesday:** swimming lessons and quick playdate with pool buddies
- **Wednesday:** library story time and park visit
- **Thursday:** soccer practice
- **Friday:** family game night or neighborhood gathering
- **Saturday:** one scheduled activity + free time
- **Sunday:** family time + prep for the week ahead

Making Space for Different Types of Connection

STRUCTURED ACTIVITIES

Think of these as your social "anchors" or regular commitments that provide consistent interaction:

- team sports (soccer, basketball, baseball)
- group lessons (art class, martial arts, dance)
- regular clubs (scouts, chess club, coding group)
- community classes (library programs, recreation center activities)

Limit structured activities to two to three per child per season. This leaves room for spontaneous play and family time.

CASUAL SOCIAL TIME

These are your "breathing spaces"; flexible, low-pressure social opportunities:

- park visits after school
- open gym at the community center
- drop-in library reading times
- playground meet ups with classmates

FAMILY CONNECTIONS

Don't forget the heart of your social calendar:

- weekly family dinner nights
- monthly game tournaments
- weekend morning pancake traditions
- regular video calls with distant relatives

Real-Life Examples

FOR YOUNG CHILDREN (AGES 3-6)

Monday morning might start with preschool, followed by a casual playground visit with classmates. Wednesday could be library story time, where your little one sees familiar faces each week. Saturday morning gymnastics class provides structured social time, while Sunday afternoon remains open for family walks or impromptu backyard play.

FOR SCHOOL-AGE KIDS (AGES 7-12)

Tuesday and Thursday afternoons might be dedicated to soccer practice, with Wednesdays saved for art class. Friday afternoons could be for rotating playdates with classmates, while Saturday mornings involve basketball games. Keep Sunday afternoons free for family time or spontaneous neighborhood play.

Making It Work

THE ART OF SAYING NO

Remember, an overscheduled family isn't a happy family. It's okay to say:

- "We're keeping Sundays for family time."
- "We can't commit to another weekly activity right now."
- "Let's plan something for next month instead."

BUILDING IN FLEXIBILITY

Life happens, and your calendar should bend rather than break:

- Keep one weekend day mostly open.
- Plan for seasonal changes in activities.
- Allow time between commitments for transitions.
- Have backup plans for outdoor activities.

Signs Your Calendar Needs Adjusting

Watch for these signals that you might need to dial things back:

- Children seem constantly tired or cranky.
- Family meals become rare.
- Homework feels rushed.
- There's no time for free play.
- Parents feel like taxi drivers more than family members.

Making Adjustments

WHEN TO SCALE BACK

- if your child isn't enjoying an activity
- when family time feels squeezed
- if preparing for activities creates stress
- when free play disappears from the schedule

WHEN TO ADD MORE

- if your child seems socially isolated
- when they express interest in new activities
- if there's too much unstructured time
- when you notice gaps in social skills

Seasonal Planning Tips

FALL

- Ease into new school routines before adding activities.
- Choose one or two main activities per child.
- Plan for earlier evenings as daylight shortens.

WINTER

- Include indoor social options.
- Plan some active indoor playdates.
- Keep weekend mornings flexible for weather changes.

SPRING

- Gradually add outdoor activities.
- Schedule around sports seasons.
- Leave room for end-of-school events.

SUMMER

- Balance camps with free time.
- Plan regular park or pool meet ups.
- Keep some weekends open for spontaneous fun.

The goal isn't to fill every moment but to create a rhythm that works for your family. Some weeks will be busier, others quieter. The key is finding a balance that lets your children grow socially while maintaining the peace and joy in your family life.

Key Takeaways

- Standing up for what's right in digital spaces often requires just one person to take the first step.
- Creating designated screen-free zones and times (like during meals, before bedtime, or in certain rooms) helps families maintain healthy digital-social balance and prioritize face-to-face connections.
- Structured family activities from cooking together to game nights to "kindness missions" provide natural opportunities for children to practice essential social skills like turn-taking, cooperation, and empathy.
- Finding the right balance in a family's social calendar means limiting structured activities (two or three per child per season), ensuring time for casual social interactions, and recognizing when to scale back if children appear constantly tired or family time feels squeezed.

Conclusion

When it comes to helping our children grow into confident, socially capable individuals, the small moments matter just as much as the big ones. Every day brings opportunities to help our kids develop the social skills they'll use throughout their lives. Whether it's learning to share toys in preschool or working through a disagreement with a friend, these experiences shape how our children will interact with others for years to come.

The beauty of teaching social skills lies in its simplicity. You don't need specialized training or complex strategies—some of the most effective teaching happens during everyday activities. Family dinner conversations, for instance, become natural training grounds for essential skills like listening, sharing experiences, and showing interest in others. When a child tells a story about their day and family members engage with questions and comments, they're learning the give-and-take of good conversation.

Our role as parents and educators goes beyond just teaching. We're actually living examples of the behaviors we hope to instill. Children are keen observers, constantly watching how we handle various social situations. When they see us navigate conflicts with patience, apologize sincerely after making mistakes, or show kindness to others, they're learning valuable lessons about social interaction. These observed moments often have a more lasting impact than any formal instruction we might provide.

Creating opportunities for social interaction is crucial. This might mean arranging playdates for younger children, encouraging participation in team sports or group activities for older ones, or simply making time for family gatherings. Each social encounter becomes a chance to practice important skills like sharing, taking turns, and reading social cues. Even challenging situations, like when a child feels left out or faces rejection, can become valuable learning experiences when handled with support and guidance.

In the classroom setting, teachers play a vital role in fostering social development. Group projects, class discussions, and team activities all serve as practical training grounds for collaboration and communication. When teachers create inclusive environments where every child's voice is valued, they help build confidence and social competence. These structured situations allow children to practice working with different personalities and managing group dynamics in a supported environment.

The digital age has added new dimensions to social skill development. Today's children need to learn how to navigate both in-person and online interactions effectively. Teaching them to be kind and respectful in digital spaces is just as important as teaching traditional social skills. This includes understanding appropriate online behavior, recognizing the impact of their digital communications, and maintaining a healthy balance between virtual and face-to-face interactions.

Handling difficult social situations requires special attention. When children face conflicts with friends, experience exclusion, or struggle with group dynamics, they need guidance to develop healthy coping strategies. These moments, though challenging, offer opportunities to teach problem-solving skills, emotional regulation, and resilience. By helping children work through these situations, we're equipping them with tools they'll use throughout their lives.

The development of empathy deserves particular focus. Teaching children to understand and care about others' feelings lays the groundwork for meaningful relationships. This can be fostered through simple practices like asking "How do you think your friend felt when that happened?" or encouraging children to consider different perspectives in various situations. When children develop strong empathy skills, they're better equipped to form lasting friendships and navigate complex social situations.

Looking toward the future, the social skills we help develop today will influence our children's success in various life areas. Strong social capabilities contribute to academic achievement, career advancement, and personal relationship satisfaction. These skills help children become effective team members, leaders, and communicators, all qualities that become increasingly valuable as they grow older.

Remember that social development is a gradual process, unique to each child. Some children naturally gravitate toward social situations, while others need more time and support to feel comfortable. The key is providing consistent encouragement while respecting each child's individual personality and pace of development. Celebrate small victories and provide gentle support during challenges, always keeping in mind that progress often happens in small steps rather than giant leaps.

As parents and educators, our investment in children's social development creates ripple effects that extend far beyond childhood. When we help children build strong social foundations, we're contributing to a future where they can form meaningful connections, work effectively with others, and navigate social situations with confidence. This investment in their social and emotional growth is truly one of the greatest gifts we can give them.

Action Steps: Your Weekly Social Skills Development Checklist

Week 1: Active Listening

- Practice making eye contact during conversations.
- Ask follow-up questions about others' stories.
- Model good listening behavior by putting away phones during discussions.

Week 2: Sharing and Turn-Taking

- Create structured opportunities for sharing during family activities.
- Practice waiting patiently during games and conversations.
- Acknowledge and praise successful sharing moments.

Week 3: Empathy Building

- Discuss characters' feelings while reading books together.
- Ask "how would you feel if…" questions during daily situations.
- Point out and discuss others' emotional cues in public settings.

Week 4: Conflict Resolution

- Teach and practice using "I feel" statements.
- Role-play common challenging social scenarios.
- Help identify multiple solutions to problems.

Week 5: Digital Communication

- Establish clear guidelines for online interactions.
- Practice writing kind and clear digital messages.
- Discuss the impact of online words and actions.

Week 6: Group Collaboration

- Arrange structured play dates or group activities.
- Assign family projects that require teamwork.
- Practice compromising and considering others' ideas.

Week 7: Social Confidence

- Create opportunities for safe social risk-taking.
- Practice introducing oneself and joining conversations.
- Celebrate attempts at new social interactions, regardless of outcome.

Week 8: Emotional Regulation

- Identify and name different emotions.
- Practice calming strategies for challenging moments.
- Create a "feelings toolkit" with coping mechanisms.

References

AllWin. (2024, July 25). 19 conflict resolution activities for students (kids & teens). AllWin Conflict Resolution Training. https://conflict-resolution-training.com/blog/conflict-resolution-activities-for-students/

Abblett, M. (2019, September 25). Tame reactive emotions by naming them. Mindful. https://www.mindful.org/labels-help-tame-reactive-emotions-naming/

Big Blue Marble Academy. Nurturing emotional security in full-time child care. (2024, September 6). Big Blue Marble Academy. https://bbmacademy.com/blog/nurturing-emotional-security-in-full-time-child-care/

Bigelow, A. E., & Power, M. (2020). Mother–infant skin-to-skin contact: short- and long-term effects for mothers and their children born full-term. Frontiers in Psychology, 11(1921). https://doi.org/10.3389/fpsyg.2020.01921

Bongiorno, L. (n.d.). Growing independence: tips for parents of toddlers and twos. NAEYC. https://www.naeyc.org/our-work/families/growing-independence-tips-parents-toddlers-and-twos

Borba, M. (2021, January 31). 3 ways to teach kids perspective taking. Michele Borba. https://micheleborba.com/building-moral-intelligence-and-character/3-ways-to-teach-perspective-taking-skills/

Boryga, A. (2023, September 22). 12 ways to help students identify their emotions. Edutopia. https://www.edutopia.org/article/12-ways-to-help-students-identify-their-emotions/

Buzanko, C. (2024, October 10). Balancing emotional support with independence in kids. Dr. Caroline Buzanko. https://drcarolinebuzanko.com/balancing-emotional-support-and-independence/

Chowdhury, M. R. (2019, August 13). Emotional regulation: 6 key skills to regulate emotions. Positive Psychology. https://positivepsychology.com/emotion-regulation/

Confident Parents Confident Kids. (2016, April 7). Cultivating compassion In our kids. Confident Parents Confident Kids. https://confidentparentsconfidentkids.org/2016/04/07/cultivating-compassion-in-our-kids/

Craig, H. (2019, February 3). 17 emotional intelligence tests and assessments (+free quizzes). Positive Psychology https://positivepsychology.com/emotional-intelligence-tests/

Curt, E. (2024, July 26). Teaching empathy for kids so they hone the skill while they're young. Kong Academy. https://www.kongacademy.org/teaching-empathy-for-kids-so-they-hone-the-skill-while-theyre-young/

de Mooij, B., Fekkes, M., Miers, A. C., van den Akker, A. L., Scholte, R. H. J., & Overbeek, G. (2023). What works in preventing emerging social anxiety: Exposure, cognitive restructuring, or a combination? Journal of Child and Family Studies, 32, 498–515. https://doi.org/10.1007/s10826-023-02536-w

Dorn, P. (2020, July 28). 8 ways to strengthen a parent-child relationship. Family Services. https://www.familyservicesnew.org/news/8-ways-to-strengthen-a-parent-child-relationship/

Everyday Speech. (2023, August 21). Developing empathy: Understanding the importance of perspective taking goals. Everyday Speech. https://everydayspeech.com/sel-implementation/developing-empathy-understanding-the-importance-of-perspective-taking-goals/

Fuller, L. (2024, February 16). 5 fun ways to use an emotions card deck with kids. C2C 2023. https://www.challengetochangeinc.com/post/5-fun-ways-to-use-an-emotions-card-deck-with-kids?srsltid=AfmBOor0EhlLlprSwf24qmkvx8WUVUex7xytcnicsITFMBEisvhqfMeM

Hanigan, A. (2024, August 27). The effects of screen time on children: The latest research parents should know. Children's Health Hub. https://health.choc.org/the-effects-of-screen-time-on-children-the-latest-research-parents-should-know/

Hutchison, M. (2024, March 19). 5 strategies for building positive relationships with children in early childhood education. Lillio.com. https://www.lillio.com/blog/5-strategies-for-building-positive-relationships-with-children-in-early-childhood-education

Jacobson, R. (2017, October 17). Teaching kids about boundaries. Child Mind Institute. https://childmind.org/article/teaching-kids-boundaries-empathy/

Larrazabal, M. (2024). Importance of social interaction. Better Speech. https://www.betterspeech.com/post/importance-of-social-interaction-in-children

Levine, A., & Philips, L. (2022). How to build independence in preschoolers. Child Mind Institute. https://childmind.org/article/how-to-build-independence-in-preschoolers/

Luthi, K. (2024, October 17). Bonding: fostering mother-infant connections. Soteria Mental Health. https://www.soteriamentalhealth.org/bonding-fostering-mother-infant-connections/

Malik, F., & Marwaha, R. (2022, September 18). Developmental stages of social emotional development in children. National Library of Medicine; StatPearls Publishing. https://www.ncbi.nlm.nih.gov/books/NBK534819/

Mcroy, K., Gerde, H. K., & Linscott, L. (2023). A three-step approach to help children navigate conflict. NAEYC. https://www.naeyc.org/resources/pubs/tyc/fall2023/three-step-approach

Mesman, E., Vreeker, A., & Hillegers, M. (2021). Resilience and mental health in children and adolescents. Current Opinion in Psychiatry, 34(6). (586-592). https://doi.org/10.1097/yco.0000000000000741

Miller, K. (2019, July 4). How can we best teach kids compassion in education? (+ 21 Activities). Positive Psychology. https://positivepsychology.com/compassion-for-kids/

Morris, A. S., Silk, J. S., Steinberg, L., Myers, S. S., & Robinson, L. R. (2007). The role of the family context in the development of emotion regulation. Social Development, 16(2), 361–388. https://doi.org/10.1111/j.1467-9507.2007.00389.x

Quinn, D. (2023, July 27). Generational trauma: 13+ effective ways to break the cycle. Sandstone Care. https://www.sandstonecare.com/blog/generational-trauma/

Seligman, L. D., & Ollendick, T. H. (2021). Cognitive-behavioral therapy for anxiety disorders in youth. Child and Adolescent Psychiatric Clinics of North America, 20(2), 217–238. https://doi.org/10.1016/j.chc.2011.01.003

Souders, B. (2019, April 9). Positive reinforcement for kids: 11+ examples for parents. Positive Psychology. https://positivepsychology.com/parenting-positive-reinforcement/

Strand, P. S., Vossen, J. J., & Savage, E. (2019). Culture and child attachment patterns: a behavioral systems synthesis. Perspectives on Behavior Science, 42(4), 835–850. https://doi.org/10.1007/s40614-019-00220-3

Wilson, D., & Conyers, M. (2017, January 4). 4 proven strategies for teaching empathy. Edutopia. https://www.edutopia.org/article/4-proven-strategies-teaching-empathy-donna-wilson-marcus-conyers/

Woodsmall Law Group. (2024, July 20). Early intervention strategies for At-Risk children. Woodsmall Law Group Articles. https://www.woodsmalllawgroup.com/blog/early-intervention-strategies-for-at-risk-children/

Woolf, N. (n.d.). 6 strategies to increase parent engagement in SEL. Panorma Education. https://www.panoramaed.com/blog/6-strategies-parent-engagement-social-emotional-learning

Xu, X., Han, W., & Liu, Q. (2023). Peer pressure and adolescent mobile social media addiction: Moderation analysis of self-esteem and self-concept clarity. Frontiers in Public Health, 11(11). https://doi.org/10.3389/fpubh.2023.1115661

Made in the USA
Columbia, SC
17 June 2025